Dovenel
anree Dee

Forming a
LIMITED
COMPANY

Forming a
LIMITED
COMPANY

FIFTH EDITION

PATRICIA CLAYTON

KOGAN
PAGE

Acknowledgement

The forms are Crown copyright and are reproduced with the permission of the Controller of Her Majesty's Stationery Office.

The author acknowledges the kind assistance of Companies House, Cardiff, in the preparation of this book.

While every care has been taken to ensure the accuracy of this work, no responsibility for loss occasioned to any person acting or refraining from action as a result of any statement in it can be accepted by the author or publisher.

First published in 1990
Second edition 1991
Third edition 1992, reprinted with revisions 1993
Fourth edition 1994, reprinted with revisions 1995
Fifth edition 1996, reprinted with revisions 1996
Reprinted 1997

Kogan Page Limited
120 Pentonville Road
London N1 9JN

© Patricia Clayton 1990, 1991, 1992, 1994, 1996

British Library Cataloguing in Publication Data
A CIP record for this book is available from the British Library.

ISBN 0–7494–1940–7

Printed and bound in Great Britain by Biddles Ltd, Guildford and King's Lynn.

◀ CONTENTS ▶

Preface   **9**

1. Why a Limited Company?   **11**
Choices 11; Why a limited company? 11; What sort of company? 11;
Advantages of trading as a limited company 12

2. Forming a Private Limited Company   **18**
Choosing your company name 18; Consumer Credit Act 1974 20; Trade
Marks 20; Trading names 20; Displaying the company's name 20;
Documents to be completed 20; The Memorandum of Association 26; The
Articles of Association 29; Duties and fees payable 32; Incorporation 32;
Pre-incorporation contracts 33; Transfer of existing business to your
company 33

3. Capital   **37**
Corporate capital 37; Increasing the company's capital 38; The share
premium account 40; Reducing the company's capital 40; Company
borrowings: mortgages, charges and debentures 41; Registration of charges
42; The Consumer Credit Act 46

4. Directors   47

Who is a director? 47; Who can be a director? 47; Appointment of directors 48; Retirement and removal 48; The board of directors 48; Directors as employees 52; Directors' duties 52; Fiduciary duty 53; Directors as agents 53; Company contracts 54; Borrowing from the company 54; Money-lending companies 54; Loans, guarantees, security for loans and advances 54; Connected persons 55; Loans to employees 55; The Consumer Credit Act 1974 55; Use of company assets 55; Disclosure 56; Fines and penalties 56; Share dealings 56; Skill and care 57; Delegation 57; Statutory duties 57; Directors' liability 58; Employers' duties 59; The directors, the company and the shareholders 59; Directors and outsiders 59; Business leases 60; Commercial contracts 61; Insurance 61; Disqualification 61

5. Running the Company   63

The registered office 63; Displaying the company name 63; Business letters and other documentation 64; Directors 64; Company secretary 64; The statutory books 65; Annual return 66; The accounts 67; Disclosing the accounts 78; Auditors 78; The company seal 79; Share issues 79; Share certificates 80; Meetings 80; The first board meeting 81; General meetings 82; Voting 82; The Annual General Meeting 82; Extraordinary General Meetings 83; Notice of meetings 83; Resolutions 84; De-regulation of private companies 84; Elective resolutions 85

6. Changes After Incorporation   86

Change of directors and secretary 86; Changing the auditors 87; Change of registered office 90; Change in the place where statutory books and other 'public' documents are kept 90; Change of name 90; Increases in capital and allotment of shares 90; The directors' authority to allot shares 97; Changes in the Memorandum of Association 97; Changes in the Articles of Association 99; Changing the accounting reference date 99; Striking the company off the Register 99

7. Insolvency   **101**

When a company is insolvent 101; Voluntary striking off 102; Voluntary arrangements: compositions and schemes of arrangement 102; Administration orders 103; Receivership 103; Receivers and directors 104; Winding up 104; Voluntary winding up 104; Voluntary liquidation 105; Distribution 106; Creditors' rights 106; Dissolution in a voluntary liquidation 106; Compulsory winding up 106; Fines and penalties 107; Voidable transactions: preferences and transactions at an undervalue 108; Dissolution in compulsory winding up 109; Restriction on use of the company name 109

8. The Ready-Made Company   **110**

Appendices

Appendix 1. Notes for Guidance on Company Names   **113**

Appendix 2. Documents to be Filed on Incorporation by a Private Limited   **119**
Liability Company

Appendix 3. Documents which must be Lodged with the Registrar   **120**

Appendix 4. Books, Registers and Documents which must be Available for   **141**
Inspection and of which Copies or Extracts can be Requisitioned

Appendix 5. Notice of First Annual General Meeting: Notice of Meeting: **146**
Resolutions: Members' Agreement to Short Notice of General
Meeting and/or of Special Resolution: Notes on Printing of Certain
Documents: Elective Resolution: Form of Proxy

Appendix 6. Useful Addresses   **157**

◀ PREFACE ▶

This is a guide for the aspiring entrepreneur starting in business and for those already running a small unincorporated business who are looking towards expansion. It explains what a private limited liability company is and the protection and advantages of trading with limited liability.

Chapter 1 describes corporate structure and its advantages and explains the procedure for incorporation and registration. Chapter 2 deals with formation and Chapter 3 covers capital structure. Directors' powers and responsibilities are dealt with in Chapter 4, and Chapters 5 and 6 deal with organisation and administration. Since some consideration must be given to what happens if things go wrong, Chapter 7 summarises the repercussions of insolvency, when the real protection given by limited liability comes into its own, and the final chapter sets out the procedure for buying a ready-made 'off the shelf' company. The English version of the various forms and documents regulating company life referred to in the text are reproduced in the relevant chapters.

This book is a guide to incorporation of English and Welsh private limited companies but the Companies Acts apply to Scotland with minor adaptations to take into account the requirements of Scottish law. Company legislation in Northern Ireland and Eire has essentially followed the Companies Acts, including changes introduced by EU legislation.

The law stated is at 31 May 1996 and is based on the Companies Acts

1985 and 1989 and the Insolvency Act 1986 but changes introduced by the 1989 Act are still being implemented. There are new forms and new fees. However, this book is intended as a guide, not a blueprint for survival, and you are advised to check with Companies House or take expert advice before forming your private limited company and making major decisions about its future.

◄ CHAPTER 1 ►

WHY A LIMITED COMPANY?

Your business structure is basic to the way you operate: it is the legal framework which determines your share of profits and losses and your responsibilities to business associates, investors, creditors and employees.

Business structure

Choices

You have three options: operating as a sole trader – running a one-man business – joining up with partners or trading as a limited liability company.

Why a limited company?

Incorporating business activities into a company confers life on the business as a 'separate legal person'. Profits and losses are the company's and it has its own debts and obligations. The business continues despite the resignation, death or bankruptcy of management and shareholders and it offers the ideal vehicle for expansion and the participation of outside investors.

What sort of company?

Options on choosing a type of company

Over 95 per cent of companies incorporated in this country are private companies limited by shares; that is, private limited liability companies. Effectively, there were nearly a million companies listed on the Companies Register in England and Wales, including public companies, with more than 5500 listed on the Companies Register in Scotland. In the year ended 31 March 1995 more than 3000 new companies were registered in England and Wales and more than 200 in Scotland with an issued share capital of less than £5000.

The bulk of the companies' legislation, unlike the legislation of most other European Union member states, applies to both public limited companies and small director-controlled family businesses. Private companies, however, cannot offer their shares and debentures to the public but the directors are permitted to retain control by restricting transfer of shares, and some concessions have been made in the requirements for filing smaller companies' accounts and reports.

Trading as a limited company and its advantages

Advantages of trading as a limited company

The main advantages of incorporating your business activities in a limited company can be summarised as follows:

- The company has a legal existence separate from management and its members (the shareholders).
- Members' liability is limited.
- The company's name is protected.
- It has flexible borrowing powers.
- The company continues despite the death, resignation or bankruptcy of management and members.
- The interests and obligations of management are defined.
- Appointment, retirement or removal of directors is straightforward.
- New shareholders and investors can be easily assimilated.
- Employees can acquire shares.
- Approved company pension schemes usually provide better benefits than those paid under contracts with the self-employed and those in non-pensionable employment. The level of premium that directors can pay is restricted but there is no limit on the overall contributions paid by the company for the directors, although there is a maximum benefit limit imposed by the Inland Revenue Superannuation Fund Office.
- Taxation: sole traders, partners and partnerships pay income tax. Sole traders' and partners' income is taxed as the proprietors' income, regardless of how much profit is retained as working capital, and interest on loans to the business is taxed as their income. Partners are

liable personally and jointly for partnership tax and, if a partner dies, the surviving partners are responsible for partnership tax.

- Directors pay income tax and the company pays corporation tax on company profits, and with current rates of tax company profits earned and retained in the business are assessed to corporation tax at lower rates than if income tax were payable on equivalent profits earned by an unincorporated business.

Limited liability

The main and most important advantage of a private company is the protection given by limited liability. The members' – its shareholders' – only liability is for the amount unpaid on their shares. Since many private companies issue shares as fully paid, if things go wrong your only loss is the value of the shares and any loans made to the company.

You can see the advantage if you compare the position of a sole trader with two separate unincorporated businesses and one becomes insolvent. Without Companies Acts protection, the solvent business's assets can be claimed by the creditors of the unsuccessful business. With protection, the creditors usually have no claim.

Protection does not, however, extend to fraud. Company directors have a duty not knowingly to incur debts they have reason to believe the company cannot or will be unlikely to repay. If they do and the creditors lose their money, the directors and anyone else involved in the fraud can be liable and their personal liability is then without limit.

Protection of the company name

The sole trader or partnership can put their names on the door and start trading but there is no property in a name and their only real protection is under the trademarks legislation or by taking legal proceedings in a 'passing-off' action for damages to compensate for loss of goodwill.

The choice of both business and company names is restricted. Company names must be registered with the Registrar of Companies and they are protected by registration on the Registrar's Index of Company Names.

Continuity

A company has a legal existence separate from its shareholders. Once formed it has everlasting life. Directors, management and employees can only act as its agent and it is the company itself which owns property and 'signs' contracts. Shares change hands, management and the workforce may change and the company continues trading, but the sole trader's business dies with him and, in the absence of contrary agreement, a partnership is dissolved on the resignation, bankruptcy or death of a partner. The artificially created company, however, is only killed off by winding up, liquidation, by order of the court or by the Registrar of Companies.

Raising capital

Borrowing

You can increase the company's permanent capital base by a new issue of shares and a company has uniquely flexible borrowing powers.

Ordinary shares can be issued for loans, giving shareholders a right to vote and receive a share of profits by way of dividends.

You can issue **preference shares** in return for loans and defer repayment to a fixed date, the happening of a specified event or by fixing the rate of dividend. Preference shares do not usually give a right to vote at company meetings and the 'preference' signifies the holder's right to payment of interest or dividend and to preferential repayment of share capital before other classes of shareholders if the company is wound up.

Debentures provide permanent additional capital and can be issued to carry a fixed rate of interest under a fixed or floating charge on some or all of the company's assets. Debenture holders have preference with regard to repayment of capital and payment of interest in a winding up, even if the issue carries no charge on the assets.

Your bank may require to be secured by a **floating charge**. The charge 'floats' on some or all of the company's assets as they exist or change from time to time and is unique to corporate borrowings. It can cover stock in trade, book debts, furniture, equipment and machinery, as well as goodwill and other unspecified assets; its advantage is that the secured assets can be freely dealt with, mortgaged or sold in the ordinary course of business until the interest or capital is unpaid or there is any other breach of the agreement with the lender. The charge then becomes fixed and the lender can appoint a receiver.

Enterprise Investment Scheme

The scheme applies to new companies only and enables a private outside investor to make a minority investment of up to £100,000 and to obtain 20 per cent income tax relief on his stake. Relief on up to half the amount invested in any one year can be carried back to the previous tax year, provided it does not exceed £15,000. The relief is available only during the first three years of the company's business life, or by a self-employed person starting in business or incorporating business activities during the first three years' trading, and usually the investment must be for a minimum of five years. The first disposal of shares is not liable for capital gains tax and there is no restriction on the amount which is deductible in calculating the chargeable gain when the shares are sold. If there is a loss you can choose between income tax or capital gains tax relief. The scheme covers most trading, manufacturing, service, research and development, construction, retail and wholesaling business but there are some exceptions, including financial services, overseas companies and investment and property companies. Companies will be able to raise up to £1m in any 12-month period. The details are complicated and if conditions are infringed, tax relief is revoked retrospectively, interest being charged on the relief, which is taxed as a loan from the Treasury; investors should therefore take advice before proceeding.

Retaining control

The sole trader and the sole director of a single-member private company run their own show, but in a partnership or company the majority rules the business. Protection of minority shareholders under the Companies Acts, however, is hard to enforce and in practical terms is not very effective. Most transactions can be ratified, even retrospectively, by majority vote of the shareholders; if you hold 75 per cent of the voting shares, and act in good faith and in the interests of the company as a whole, the minority shareholders can only question your decisions if they can prove fraud.

You can now form, and change existing companies into, single-member private companies, thus eliminating all possibility of shareholder conflict. As sole shareholder your name and address must be set out in the register of members, together with the date of the change and a statement that the company is a single-member company. The sole member exercises the powers of the general meeting and must minute all decisions. Details of contracts between the sole member and the company must also be minuted. Where decisions are not minuted, the sole member is liable to pay a fine but the decision remains valid.

The 1989 Companies Act provides for the incorporation of partnership companies – companies whose shares are wholly or partly held by their employees – but the legislative framework is not yet in place.

Taxation

Tax

The sole trader, the partner and the director pay income tax; companies pay corporation tax.

The sole trader is and partners are personally liable to the Revenue for tax on their share of business profits. Under the new self-assessment rules retiring partners take their tax liability with them and when partners die, their tax liability passes to their estates. Income tax was formerly assessed on the partnership as a whole, but from 1997/98 partners are separately assessed to income tax on their share of profits. The partnership will, however, have to complete a Partnership (tax) Return setting out the partnership's profits or losses for tax purposes, and showing how it was divided between the partners.

Another change is that from 1996/97 self-assessment to tax for partnerships started after 5 April 1994 is based on the current tax year instead of the preceding year's income. Businesses existing before 5 April 1994 are not affected until 1997/98. Assessment under transitional provisions for the 1996/97 tax year will be based on the average profit of the two years ending on 5 April 1996 and 5 April 1997.

A director's income is taxed at source under PAYE, and interest on loans to the company and share income are included in taxable earnings. There are certain advantages if his or her salary exceeds £8500 per annum; the first £30,000 on 'golden handshakes' paid *ex gratia* or as compensation for loss of office is tax free with a reduced rate applied up to £50,000 and redundancy payments can be claimed if the company is wound up.

The company is taxed separately for corporation tax on business profits at 33 per cent but 'small companies' are taxed at the lower rate of 24 per cent; capital gains are taxed at the same rate as income, whether or not they are distributed as income. To qualify as small, the company's taxable profits must not exceed £300,000 and tapering relief applies up to £1,500,000, after which the full 33 per cent rate is payable. Capital allowances and various tax incentives for investment in small businesses have made this country a corporate tax haven, so advice should be sought to take maximum advantage of the situation.

There are tax concessions if you incorporate your business and sell it to the company as a going concern in exchange for shares, and a further concession extends to an Enterprise Investment Scheme investor's first disposal of shares in your company.

Companies pay capital transfer tax and individuals pay inheritance tax and both pay income tax on capital gains; for the most part, unless your business is very small, a director is better off than a sole trader or partner taking out the same share of profits.

◄ CHAPTER 2 ►

FORMING A PRIVATE LIMITED COMPANY

Companies must comply with the rules of corporate organisation and management contained in the Companies Acts. These apply to all companies, large and small, public and private but some concessions are given to smaller companies and it is simpler and less costly in this country than in any other major commercial centre to incorporate your business activities.

Companies Registration Office

The Registrar of Companies at the Companies Registration Office, Companies House, Crown Way, Maindy, Cardiff CF4 3UZ, and in Scotland, 37 Castle Terrace, Edinburgh EH1 2EB, deals with company registrations and the forms and documentation which the company is required to file in accordance with the companies legislation. Notes for guidance on incorporation and for some of the Companies Acts' requirements as well as the statutory forms are available from Companies House free of charge. The Registrar's staff are helpful and there is a customer care department which deals with consumer queries.

Selecting and registering a name for your company

Choosing your company name

Your brand new company's brand new name costs £20 on application for incorporation of your business activities to the Registrar of Companies.

Describing your business activities through your choice of name is effective and cheap advertising but the following restrict your choice:

- The last word of the company name must be 'limited' or 'ltd'. If your registered office is in Wales, the Welsh equivalent 'cyfyngedig' or 'cyf' may be used and company documentation must then also state in English that it is a limited company and the information must be displayed at all places where the company carries on business. Charitable or 'quasi-charitable' companies are exempt from this requirement but a 'quasi-charitable' company must indicate on its documentation that it is a limited company.
- The name must not be the same as or similar to one appearing in the Index of Names kept by the Registrar of Companies.
- Certain 'sensitive' words and expressions listed in Appendix 1 cannot be used without the consent of the Secretary of State or relevant government department. For instance, only authorised banks may use a name which might reasonably be understood to indicate they are in the business of banking.
- The name must not imply a connection with the government or a local authority.
- The name must not be offensive, nor must its use constitute a criminal offence.

Application to register the name is made to the Registrar's Cardiff or Edinburgh office. When permission is granted, the name is reserved pending the passing of a special resolution of 75 per cent of the company's shareholders confirming the name. A copy of the resolution must be sent to the Registrar, together with the registration fee. The name is not effective and may not be used until the Registrar issues the Certificate of Incorporation and permission may be withdrawn before it is issued. The directors are personally liable on contracts made on behalf of the company before issue of the Certificate, so you should allow time for the application for conditional approval to be processed as well as for any delay in sending you the Certificate permitting use of the name.

You must arrange for your own search of the Index at Companies House in London or the Registrar's offices in Cardiff and Edinburgh and it does not show pending applications. If your name is the same or 'too like' an existing company's, you may be required to change it within 12 months of registration. The time limit is extended to five years if the Secretary of State feels that he has been given misleading information or undertakings or assurances given on registration have not been met; he can direct a change of name at any time if the name is so misleading as to the nature of the company's activities that it is likely to cause harm to the public.

Consumer Credit Act 1974

Registration of the name does not imply acceptance for the purpose of this legislation. If the business requires to be licensed under the Act, you should contact the licensing branch of the Office of Fair Trading, Bromyard Avenue, Acton, London W3, to check whether the name is acceptable to them.

Trade marks

Trade marks

Acceptance of your company name does not mean that it can be used as a trade mark. To ensure that you do not infringe anyone's trade mark rights you should search the appropriate class of goods and services at the Trade Marks Registry. Trade mark rights give an automatic right of action against the infringer. Use of an unregistered name may expose you to the risk of a 'passing off' action but compensation is then payable only if the plaintiff can prove that the public has been confused.

Trading names

The restrictions on your choice of trading name are set out in Appendix 1 but otherwise almost any name is acceptable provided it is not misleading or, unless you have the consent of the Minister or relevant department, does not imply a connection with the Royal Family, government or local authority, or national or international pre-eminence.

Displaying your company name

Displaying the company's name

All company documents and stationery must carry the company's full name; its registered number and the address of its registered office must also be included on the company's letterhead. The name must be prominently displayed at the principal place of business and engraved on the company seal (see page 79) and it must not be abbreviated or amended, for instance by changing 'X & Co Ltd' to 'X and Company Limited'. It must also appear on company cheques, payment then being made 'for and on behalf of the company'. Cheques without the company name are the personal liability of the signatory.

Documentation procedure

Documents to be completed

The following documents must be completed and sent to the Registrar, so that incorporation and registration can be effected:

- The printed Memorandum of Association, signed by at least two promoters or the promoter of a single member company – the 'subscribers' to the Memorandum – who write opposite their names the number of shares they have agreed to take. They can take up any number of shares and their full names and addresses must be given and their signatures attested by one or more witnesses, giving their full name, address and occupation. Minors, that is persons under the age of 18, should not subscribe as they can repudiate the shares on or before majority. Other companies can subscribe by having a director or secretary sign on their behalf but this should be clearly stated by the signatory signing 'for and on behalf of' the corporate member.

- The printed Articles of Association dated and signed by the subscribers to the Memorandum, their signatures again being witnessed.

- A Statement of First Director(s) and Secretary and Intended Situation of Registered office (*Form 10* – see page 22). You must give details of the officers; directors must give their dates of birth and the form contains a signed consent by the first director(s) and secretary agreeing to act. The form must also be signed and dated by the subscribers to the Memorandum or by an agent acting on their behalf.

- A Declaration of Compliance with the Requirements on Application for Registration of a Company (*Form 12* – see page 25) signed and dated by the proposed director or secretary named in *Form 10*, or by a solicitor dealing with the formation of the company. The declaration must be sworn before a Commissioner for Oaths or a solicitor having the power conferred on a Commissioner for Oaths or before a Notary Public or Justice of the Peace, who must also state the place where the declaration was made and date the form.

The completed forms must be sent to the Registrar with the registration fee of £20. A same-day service for incorporation and registration costs £200.

It is at this stage that the proposed name is checked and, subject to approval of the name, the Certificate of Incorporation giving the date of signature and the registered number of the company is issued which must be put on all documents sent to the Registrar.

As from the date of issue of the Certificate, the subscribers form a body corporate – the new company – which exercises its own powers. Prior to that date, however, the company has no existence, so that any business contracts already agreed are the personal responsibility of the signatories.

C O M P A N I E S   H O U S E

10

Please complete in typescript,
or in bold black capitals.

Notes on completion appear on final page

First directors and secretary and intended situation of
registered office

Company Name in full

∗F010001H∗

Proposed Registered Office

(PO Box numbers only, are not acceptable)

Post town

County / Region   Postcode

If the memorandum is delivered by an agent
for the subscriber(s) of the memorandum
mark the box opposite and give the agent's
name and address.

Agent's Name

Address

Post town

County / Region   Postcode

Number of continuation sheets attached

Please give the name, address,
telephone number and, if available,
a DX number and Exchange of
the person Companies House should
contact if there is any query.

Tel

DX number   DX exchange

When you have completed and signed the form please send it to the
Registrar of Companies at:
Companies House, Crown Way, Cardiff, CF4 3UZ   DX 33050 Cardiff
for companies registered in England and Wales
or
Companies House, 37 Castle Terrace, Edinburgh, EH1 2EB
for companies registered in Scotland   **DX 235 Edinburgh**

Form revised March 1995

Company Secretary (see notes 1-5)

Company name [ ]

NAME *Style / Title [ ] *Honours etc [ ]

* Voluntary details

Forename(s) [ ]

Surname [ ]

Previous forename(s) [ ]

Previous surname(s) [ ]

Address [ ]

Usual residential address
For a corporation, give the
registered or principal office
address. [ ]

Post town [ ]

County / Region [ ] Postcode [ ]

Country [ ]

I consent to act as secretary of the company named on page 1

Consent signature [ ] **Date** [ ]

Directors (see notes 1-5)

Please list directors in alphabetical order

NAME *Style / Title [ ] *Honours etc [ ]

Forename(s) [ ]

Surname [ ]

Previous forename(s) [ ]

Previous surname(s) [ ]

Address [ ]

Usual residential address
For a corporation, give the
registered or principal office
address. [ ]

Post town [ ]

County / Region [ ] Postcode [ ]

Country [ ]

Day Month Year

Date of birth [ ][ ][ ] **Nationality** [ ]

Business occupation [ ]

Other directorships [ ]

[ ]

I consent to act as director of the company named on page 1

Consent signature [ ] **Date** [ ]

23

Directors (continued) (see notes 1-5)

NAME	*Style / Title	*Honours etc

* Voluntary details

Forename(s)	
Surname	
Previous forename(s)	
Previous surname(s)	

Address

Usual residential address
For a corporation, give the registered or principal office address.

Post town	
County / Region	Postcode
Country	

	Day Month Year	
Date of birth		Nationality
Business occupation		
Other directorships		

I consent to act as director of the company named on page 1

Consent signature		**Date**

This section must be signed by
Either

an agent on behalf of all subscribers	Signed		Date
Or the subscribers	Signed		Date
(*i.e those who signed as members on the memorandum of association).*	Signed		Date
	Signed		Date
	Signed		Date
	Signed		Date
	Signed		Date

COMPANIES HOUSE

Please complete in typescript, or in bold black capitals.

Declaration on application for registration

12

Company Name in full

F 0 1 2 0 0 1 J

I,

of

† Please delete as appropriate.

do solemnly and sincerely declare that I am a [Solicitor engaged in the formation of the company][person named as director or secretary of the company in the statement delivered to the Registrar under section 10 of the Companies Act 1985]† and that all the requirements of the Companies Act 1985 in respect of the registration of the above company and of matters precedent and incidental to it have been complied with.

And I make this solemn Declaration conscientiously believing the same to be true and by virtue of the Statutory Declarations Act 1835.

Declarant's signature

Declared at

the   day of

One thousand nine hundred and ninety

❶ Please print name.   before me ❶

Signed   **Date**

A Commissioner for Oaths or Notary Public or Justice of the Peace or Solicitor

Please give the name, address, telephone number and, if available, a DX number and Exchange of the person Companies House should contact if there is any query.

Tel

DX number   DX exchange

When you have completed and signed the form please send it to the Registrar of Companies at:
Companies House, Crown Way, Cardiff, CF4 3UZ   **DX 33050 Cardiff**
for companies registered in England and Wales
or
Companies House, 37 Castle Terrace, Edinburgh, EH1 2EB
for companies registered in Scotland   **DX 235 Edinburgh**

Form revised March 1995

The Memorandum of Association

The company's constitution is contained in two documents: the Memorandum and Articles of Association. The Memorandum sets out the company's basic constitution and its powers and duties as a legal person. The Companies (Tables A to F) Regulations 1985 (1985 SI No 805 as amended) available from Her Majesty's Stationery Office (HMSO) give a standard form of Memorandum and Articles; draft forms for both the Memorandum and Articles of Association suitably modified for use by a private limited company can be obtained from law and specialist stationers, which can be further modified for your purposes before you apply for registration.

The Memorandum of Association must state:

- **The company's name**: unless it is registered or re-registered with unlimited liability, the last word of the name, if it is trading for profit, must be 'limited' or 'ltd' or the Welsh equivalent; a Welsh company can file its Memorandum and Articles in Welsh, together with an English translation and you should check with Companies House to see if an English translation is still required.

- **That the registered office is in England, Wales or Scotland** (London, Cardiff or Edinburgh is also acceptable): this establishes the company's domicile which, unless you can show that management and control are elsewhere, means that the company operates under British law and pays British tax.

  The registered office need not be the place at which you carry on business and it is often convenient to use your accountant's or solicitor's address. It is, however, the address to which important and official documents are sent, including service of legal proceedings, so it is important to receive prompt notification of receipt of any documents.

  The address must be filed with the Registrar when you start business or within 15 days of incorporation, whichever is the earlier date. It can be changed, provided you stay in England and Wales or in Scotland, but the Registrar must be notified within 15 days of the change.

  The registered office address, the place of registration and the company's registered number must be put on all business documentation.

- **The objects for which the company is formed**: this clause sets out the objects for which the company is incorporated and specifies its powers. If the company pursues any other object or goes beyond the specified powers, it is acting *ultra vires* (beyond the powers of) the company.

Under the 1989 Companies Act a general commercial company's bare statement that the object of the company is to carry on any trade or business whatsoever *and* that the company has power to do all such things as are incidental to the carrying on of its trade or business, is sufficient on the basis that the validity of any act done by the company 'shall not be called into question on the ground of lack of capacity'. However, the legislation has not yet been tested in the courts and it may therefore be advisable to include provisions similar to those required under the earlier law, which require the company's objectives and powers to be set out in full. 'To make a profit' is implied but everything else must be specified.

The **objects clause** is divided into a number of sub-clauses. The first covers the main business activity and should state clearly and fully all the businesses and activities that it is anticipated the company will undertake. The second sub-clause is usually a 'mopping up' clause which covers any other business which in the opinion of the directors may advantageously or conveniently be carried on in conjunction with the company's main business.

If, however, the company has been formed for a specific money-making venture, this is its main object and if it does not produce a profit and you have included nothing else, the company must be wound up. The objects clause can be changed but only to extend or vary the approach to the specified business activities, to restrict or abandon them or to sell out to another company. Alterations must be approved by a special resolution of 75 per cent of the shareholders and can be cancelled by the court on the application of a minority of share and debenture holders within 21 days of the resolution.

It is therefore advisable to include everything you might wish to do, setting out several possibilities and stating that any of them can be the main and independent object of the company, in order that your search for profit can be flexible. The standard form is by including a clause stating that 'every object shall be considered a separate and independent main object and none of the objects specified shall be deemed to be subsidiary or auxiliary to any other'.

Following sub-clauses enable the company and the directors to buy, sell and lease property; to construct buildings, plant and machinery;

to borrow and to lend; to acquire patents; to issue shares and debentures; to purchase shares in other companies; to enter into partnership and acquire other businesses; to sell the undertaking of the company; to draw bills of exchange and negotiable instruments; to establish associations and clubs to benefit directors and employees; to distribute property to members and to do all such other things as may be deemed incidental or conducive to the attainment of the main objects.

The directors cannot borrow or invest on behalf of the company unless they are given the power to do so in the **objects clause**, so it should be framed to give the widest possible powers. They can also be authorised to make charitable, political or other contributions, although it is advisable to impose some control on excessive philanthropy and speculation by providing that no director can act without the approval of a majority of the board.

However wide your **objects clause**, some acts and transactions may still be *ultra vires* the company and of senior management. Since entry into the EU, however, transactions with third parties acting in good faith and not specifically aware of a restriction bind the company which can, in some circumstances, turn to the director or senior employee for compensation.

Limited liability

- **That the liability of the member(s) is limited**: this means that if the company is insolvent, the shareholders are liable to creditors for only the amount still owing on their shares; if they are paid for in full, they have no further liability. This applies to all the shareholders, including directors and management although they may have a separate liability to the company as officers.

If the company continues trading for more than six months with only one shareholder, he has sole liability for company debts incurred during that period if he knows he is the only shareholder.

Capital, share issues etc

- **The amount of initial nominal (or authorised) capital and how it is divided into shares**: this clause states the capital, how it is divided into shares and the nominal value of each share, usually £1.

The percentage of the capital subscribed in cash or asset value is called the issued share capital. Any balance remaining unpaid is the uncalled capital and the shareholders' liability is limited to this amount if the company goes into liquidation. References to share capital in the company's letterhead must quote the issued/paid up amount, not the nominal figure.

Class rights, attaching to different classes of shares (see below), may also be set out in the Memorandum but are usually set out in the Articles.

- **The name(s) of the subscriber(s)**: your new company must have at least two subscribers or signatories to the Memorandum in the **association clause** which states that they want to be formed into a company and that they agree to take out at least one share each. If you intend to trade as a single-member company, yours is the only signature required as subscriber to the Memorandum.

The Articles of Association

The Articles deal with your internal organisation, the company's relationship with shareholders and their relationship with each other, the issue of share capital, the appointment and the detailed powers of directors and proceedings at meetings.

The 1985 Regulations contain a set of 118 standard Articles which are designed for large public companies as well as the small private company, so they are usually adopted with modifications. For instance, you may wish more specifically to define and restrict the directors' borrowing powers by requiring that loans over a specified amount must be approved by a majority of the board.

Classes of shares

You may want to divide shareholdings into several classes of shares, with different rights attached to each class. The ordinary shares usually carry voting rights and a share of profits (payable as dividend) but shares can be issued carrying increased voting rights or priority in right to dividend or repayment of original capital if the company is wound up. The Articles can set out how rights can be altered or new rights or classes of shares created and unless they state otherwise, the changes can then be made by passing an ordinary (majority vote) resolution.

Restrictions on issue of shares

The existing shareholders have a statutory right of pre-emption, that is, the right of first refusal, over most new share issues, so they must first be offered to the existing shareholders *pro rata* (in proportion) to their holding at a specified date. The shareholders must be notified in writing of the offer which must be open for at least 21 days. Your private company's Articles, however, can instead give the directors a discretion on allotment

Articles of Association

Shares

of shares (refer to the standard Articles contained in Table A). If the directors are given authority to allot shares, their authority must be renewed five years from the date of incorporation or from the date of adoption of the Article.

Restriction on share transfers

In order to retain control, directors of private companies usually want to restrict the transfer of shares; this must be done by adding a special provision to the standard Articles, which normally provides that the directors may, at their discretion and without having to give a reason, decline to register any transfer of shares.

Often a right of pre-emption (right of first refusal – see above) is also given to the existing shareholders when a member wishes to sell his shares. The appropriate Article will set out the detailed procedure for the offer and refusal, including time limits and the method of valuation, with recourse to arbitration if a price cannot be agreed. It should be carefully drafted at the outset, because although the Articles can be changed it may be more difficult to agree the terms at a later stage. The small family company's family directors' domestic problems can have a drastic effect on business decisions and you may by then also have to consider the interests of outside shareholders.

The basic decision is whether or not the directors should be able to block transfers within and outside the family during a shareholder's lifetime and afterwards, and much depends on the personal circumstances of the promoters.

Purchase by the company of its own shares

Companies can now buy their own shares and assist anyone else to buy them, provided the company's assets are not thereby reduced or, to the extent of the reduction, the finance comes out of distributable profits, that is, profits available for payment of dividends.

Table A includes this provision but the procedure is complicated and there are tax implications, so professional advice should be sought before you take action.

Directors

First directors are named in the statement filed on registration and the Articles usually set out the method of electing subsequent directors, and specify the maximum and minimum number of directors. Table A specifies a minimum of two but a private company may operate with one director, although he may not then be the company secretary.

Anyone can be a director of a private company, provided that he or she is not a bankrupt or disqualified from acting as a director under the Insolvency Act. The Articles usually disqualify anyone who is of unsound mind or who is absent from board meetings for more than six months without consent. A company can be a director of another company; directors need not hold shares but the Articles can provide that they be required to hold a specific shareholding.

Usually a third of the directors retire and stand for re-appointment by rotation each year but the Articles can make provision for life-time directorships.

The Articles covering directors' appointment and removal, however, can be changed by ordinary (majority vote) resolution of the shareholders and the resolution overrides any service agreement made between the director and the company, although the director can claim compensation for loss of office on breach of the agreement. The director's position can be safeguarded by giving him sufficient special voting rights on shares owned to outweigh the votes of other shareholders.

Directors' powers

The majority shareholders run the company but in practice the real power is with the majority of the board of directors, who usually exercise their powers through resolutions passed at board meetings. In larger companies the board deals with general policy; day-to-day decisions are left to the managing director and committees of directors. The smaller company works in the same way but in practice decisions are often made by all the directors on a daily basis.

Table A provides that company business shall be managed by the directors and in addition that the directors may exercise all the powers of the company (contained in the Memorandum) to borrow money, mortgage its property and issue securities. However, you may want to add a provision limiting the total amount of debt which the directors can incur on behalf of the company without the prior consent of shareholders.

Directors' salaries

Directors' remuneration and their expenses must be authorised by an appropriate provision in the Articles. Table A provides for payment of such remuneration as the company may by ordinary resolution determine and payment of travelling, hotel and other expenses properly incurred in connection with attendance at directors' and company meetings. Directors are advised also to agree a full service contract with the company, covering salary, share of profits and/or bonuses and reimbursement of expenses to safeguard their position.

General provisions

Other standard articles cover, for instance, the company's lien on shares for the balance unpaid; making calls on members for moneys payable on shares; forfeiture of shares where calls have not been paid; meetings, notice of meetings and procedure at meetings, including voting procedure; keeping of minutes and appointment and removal of officers; declaration and payment of dividends; winding up; indemnity of directors and use of the company seal (see page 78).

The 1989 Companies Act dispensed with the need for a company seal and the signatures of two directors, or a director and the company secretary, signing for and on behalf of the company has the same effect as if the document had been executed under seal. Your standard Articles will require use of a seal and, at the time of writing, the only evidence of title to a share certificate is a certificate executed under seal. An alternative scheme to abolish share certificates so that title can be transferred via computer accounts is not yet in operation.

Duties and fees payable

£20 is payable to the Registrar of Companies when lodging documents on formation and the fee stamp is affixed on the Memorandum of Association. Same-day incorporation costs £200.

Certificate of Incorporation

Incorporation

The company exists from the date that the Companies Registration Office issues the Certificate of Incorporation, which is numbered, dated and signed. The name can be changed after incorporation but not the registered number, so if you want to trace a company you should quote the number.

Pre-incorporation contracts

When you organise the business with a view to transferring it to a company, you become a promoter and you and your co-promoters are personally liable in any transaction entered into on behalf of your future company before incorporation, unless you make other specific provision in the agreement. You should therefore contract on the basis that you will cease to be liable once the contract is put before the board or general meeting on incorporation, whether or not the company adopts the transaction. Once it is adopted, the contract is replaced by a draft agreement, which is executed by the company after incorporation.

Transfer of existing business to your company

Existing business can be transferred to your company

You can sell your business to the company for shares issued at par (face value). Assets and liabilities are taken over by the company and no capital gains tax is chargeable provided the only payment is the issue of shares.

A formal transfer agreement should be executed transferring existing assets and liabilities to the company on incorporation, but professional advice should be sought as to the tax and legal aspects of transfer. It is advisable to provide a proper valuation of the assets transferred, although you are not obliged to do so and you should formally disclose details of the transactions to shareholders even if this is a formality at this early stage when the company may have only one or two shareholders. Full details should be put on file and the sale should be properly minuted when the transaction is adopted at the first general meeting.

The sale agreement or prescribed form of details of the sale and *Form 88(3)* – see page 34 – must be lodged with the Registrar within one month of the transaction. A stamp duty of 1 per cent *ad valorem* (according to value) is payable on transfer of some assets but there is no charge to duty if the total consideration does not exceed £30,000 and the agreement contains a Certificate of Value, which certifies that 'the transaction hereby effected does not form part of a larger transaction or a series of transactions in respect of which the amount or value or aggregate amount or value of the consideration exceeds £30,000'.

G

COMPANIES FORM No. 88(3)

Particulars of a contract relating to shares allotted as fully or partly paid up otherwise than in cash

88(3)

Pursuant to section 88(3) of the Companies Act 1985

Please do not
write in
this margin

Note: This form is only for use when the contract has not been reduced to writing

Please complete
legibly, preferably
in black type, or
bold block lettering

To the Registrar of Companies
(Address overleaf)

For official use

Company number

Please do not
write in the space
below. For Inland
Revenue use only

The particulars must be stamped with the same stamp duty as would have been payable if the contract had been reduced to writing. A reduced rate of ad valorem duty may be available if this form is properly certified at the appropriate amount.

Name of company

* insert full name
of company

*

gives the following particulars of a contract which has not been reduced to writing

1 The number of shares allotted as fully or partly paid up otherwise than in cash	
2 The nominal value of each such share	£
3a The amount of such nominal value to be considered as paid up on each share otherwise than in cash	£
b The value of each share allotted i.e. the nominal value and any premium	£
c The amount to be considered as paid up in respect of b	£
4 If the consideration for the allotment of such shares is services, or any consideration other than that mentioned below in 8, state the nature and amount of such consideration, and the number of shares allotted	

Presentor's name address and
reference (if any):

For official Use

Capital Section

Post room

Page 1

34

| 5 If the allotment is a bonus issue, state the amount of reserves capitalised in respect of this issue | £ | |

| 6 If the allotment is made in consideration of the release of a debt, e.g., a director's loan account, state the amount released | £ | |

| 7 If the allotment is made in connection with the conversion of loan stock, state the amount of stock converted in respect of this issue | £ | |

8 If the allotment is made in satisfaction or part satisfaction of the purchase price of property, give below:

a brief description of property:

b full particulars of the manner in which the purchase price is to be satisfied	£	p
Amount of consideration payable in cash or bills		
Amount of consideration payable in debentures, etc......		
Amount of consideration payable in shares		
Liabilities of the vendor assumed by the purchaser:		
Amounts due on mortgages of freeholds and/or leaseholds including interest to date of sale		
Hire purchase etc debts in respect of goods acquired ...		
Other liabilities of the vendor,...............................		
Any other consideration		

Page 2

35

Please do not write in this margin

* Where such properties are sold subject to mortgage, the gross value should be shown

9 Give full particulars in the form of the following table, of the property which is the subject of the sale, showing in detail how the total purchase price is apportioned between the respective heads:

£

Legal estates in freehold property and fixed plant and machinery and other fixtures thereon* ....

Legal estates in leasehold property* ....

Fixed plant and machinery on leasehold property (including tenants', trade and other fixtures) ....

Equitable interests in freehold or leasehold property* ....

Loose plant and machinery, stock-in-trade and other chattels (plant and machinery should not be included under this head unless it was in actual state of severance on the date of the sale) ....

Goods, wares and merchandise subject to hire purchase or other agreements (written down value) ....

Goodwill and benefit of contracts ....

Patents, designs, trademarks, licences, copyrights, etc.

Book and other debts ....

Cash in hand and at bank on current account, bills, notes, etc ....

Cash on deposit at bank or elsewhere ....

Shares, debentures and other investments ....

Other property ....

‡ Insert Director, Secretary, Administrator, Administrative Receiver or Receiver (Scotland) as appropriate

Signed   Designation‡   Date

§ This certificate must be signed by the persons to whom the shares have been allotted, as well as by an officer of the company.

Certificate of value§

It is certified that the transaction effected by the contract does not form part of a larger transaction or series of transactions in respect of which the amount or value, or aggregate amount or value, of the consideration exceeds £

Signed   Date

Page 3   Signed   Date

◀ CHAPTER 3 ▶

CAPITAL

The limited liability company is structured for expansion; once incorporated, your business easily assimilates additional participants and capital and you can retain control as the majority shareholder.

Corporate capital

The company can build up a complicated capital structure and a whole range of special terms describes capital contributions.

Initial capital contributions

Your company's capital structure

When two directors each contribute £400 to form a company with a nominal or authorised capital of £1000, each taking 500 shares with a par or nominal value of £1 each, that £800 is the company's paid-up capital for 1000 shares in the company. The balance of £200 outstanding is the uncalled capital. This can be called on by the company at any time, in accordance with the terms of the Articles, unless it is later decided (by special resolution) to make all or part of it reserve capital which is only called on if the company goes into liquidation.

Nominal capital is the total amount of share capital which the Memorandum authorises the company to issue and any reference to capital on business documents must refer to the issued paid-up capital.

Shares

Your contribution of capital gives you a right to a share of distributed profits but it does not necessarily fix the proportion to which you are entitled.

Payment can be in cash or in kind, including goodwill, know-how or an undertaking to do work or perform services for the company or a third party.

The **ordinary shares** issued on incorporation give you a claim to income on equal parts of the company's net assets. If you later issue **preference shares**, their preferential rights must be met before the ordinary share dividend is paid.

Increasing capital

Increasing the company's capital

You can increase the company's nominal capital by issuing more shares if this is permitted by the Articles. The issue must be authorised by resolution of the company in general meeting in accordance with the relevant Article. If there is no provision for a new issue, an appropriate Article can be added (by special resolution of three-quarters of the shareholders).

The new capital can be by issue of ordinary, preferred or even deferred shares, paid for on instalment terms; if the Memorandum does not permit this, however, you will have to vote on an appropriate amendment.

Notice of the increase must be sent to the Registrar within 15 days of the passing of the resolution, together with a copy of the Minutes of the Meeting, the authorising resolution and the printed amended Memorandum and/or Article.

Pre-emptive rights
Existing shareholders have pre-emptive rights to new issues in proportion to their shareholding, unless this is excluded in the Articles, payment is not in cash, or the shares carry a fixed dividend, or the directors are authorised to allot the shares.

Directors' authority to allot shares
The directors' authority to allot shares must be contained in the Articles or granted by the shareholders by an ordinary majority resolution in

general meeting. It can be conditional or unconditional and lasts for a maximum of five years, renewable for a further five years.

Rights attached to shares, including the right to dividend, depend on the terms of the company's Memorandum and Articles. If you attach the right to vote at general meetings to only one class of shares, the company can be given a wide capital base but management retains control.

Once rights are attached to shares, whether by amendment to the Articles or otherwise, rights can only be varied by the consent of the shareholders affected, however small the group.

Class rights stated to be unalterable in the Memorandum can only be varied with the consent of all the shareholders but, if they will not agree a change, it may be possible to vary them by way of a 'scheme of arrangement' (see page 97).

Details of some share issues carrying special rights which are not stated in the Memorandum or Articles must be filed with the Registrar within one month of allotment. It is therefore advisable to seek specialist advice if you are considering such issues.

Preference shares come in all guises but they all have some preference over other classes of shares in their right to dividend and/or repayment of capital.

Preference shares

Preference dividends are paid at a fixed percentage rate on the price of the share before anything is paid to ordinary shareholders; you can issue several classes of preference shares, ranking one behind the other in their right to dividend. Their dividends are cumulative unless the Memorandum or Articles state that they are not, so that arrears must be paid before the ordinary dividend is paid. If they are stated to be non-cumulative, a dividend passed is a dividend lost for ever. Participating preference or preferred ordinary shareholders receive their share of any surplus distributed profits after the preference and ordinary share dividends have been paid.

If the company goes into liquidation, the accumulated arrears of preference dividends are payable after the creditors are paid off.

Ordinary shareholders are then entitled to the return of capital, in proportion to the nominal value of their shares, unless the Memorandum and Articles give the preference shareholders priority to capital. Surplus assets are usually split between ordinary and participating preference shareholders.

Redeemable preference shares are similar to debentures (see page 41) and advice should be sought before issue.

Share warrants are usually issued only to holders of fully paid-up shares but they can be attached to, for instance, a debenture issue, with the option to convert them into fully paid-up shares at a future date. They usually pay dividends when the coupon attached to the warrant is sent to the company. Unlike share certificates, however, they are negotiable, so if they are lost or stolen the original holder may have no rights against the company. Sometimes voting rights are attached but the Articles may only permit a vote on deposit of the warrant. Companies usually contact holders by newspaper advertisement only, so they often miss meetings and may not receive dividends promptly.

Share premium account

The share premium account

If you are trading profitably and have built up reserves, the true value of shares is increased. If new shares are issued at more than the par (nominal) value of previously issued shares of the same class, the premium must be transferred to a share premium account, which becomes part of the company's capital. This cannot then be distributed without the consent of the court, unless it is used for a bonus or rights issue, or to provide a premium for the redemption of redeemable preference shares or debentures, but it can be used to write off the expenses of another issue.

Reducing capital

Reducing the company's capital

You can reduce the company's capital by buying back its shares, provided you have an appropriate provision in the Articles. The procedure is complicated and the penalties for non-compliance include imprisonment and/or a fine, so you should take legal and financial advice before taking action.

Company borrowings: mortgages, charges and debentures

A trading company can borrow and give security without a specific provision in its Memorandum and Articles but you should ensure that your company has the widest possible borrowing and investment powers to avoid problems with lenders and shareholders and specifically exclude the provisions of Table A which restrict the borrowing power of both the company and the directors.

A money-lending company can lodge its own shares as security in a transaction entered into by the company in the ordinary course of its business and any company can mortgage partly paid-up shares for the balance remaining unpaid.

Debentures

You can raise additional capital by a debenture issue. The debenture itself is a document given by the company to the debenture holder as evidence of a mortgage or charge on company assets for a loan with interest. The holder is a creditor of the company, but often holds one of a series of debentures with similar rights attached to them or is one of a class of debenture holders whose security is transferable (like shares) or negotiable (like warrants).

Fixed charges and floating charges

If the debenture is secured by specific assets, the charge is fixed. A charge over all the company's assets – which will include stock in trade, goodwill and so on – is a floating charge, as the security changes from time to time. A floating charge, which allows the company freely to deal with business assets, automatically crystallises into a fixed charge if the company is wound up or stops trading, or if it is in default under the terms of the loan and the debenture holder takes steps to enforce the security.

You can create separate fixed and floating charges and the floating charge is always enforceable after a fixed charge, in whatever order they were made, unless it prohibits a loan with prior rights on the security of the fixed assets and the lender under the fixed charge knows of the restriction. Banks usually include this provision in their lending agreements covering the company's overdraft, so that you may have difficulties if you run into a basic liquidity problem, as cheques paid into the account after a company ceases trading may be fraudulent preferences (see page 60).

Charges must be registered

Registration of charges

All charges, which include mortgages, created by the company must be registered with the Registrar within 21 days of creation. Your bank's charge on credit balances is not registrable unless it is charged to a third party.

The requirement covers charges made as security for debentures, floating charges on the company's assets including a charge on book debts, as well as charges on any interest in land or goods (except, in the case of goods, where the chargee is entitled to possession of the goods or of a document of title to them), and charges on intangible moveable property (in Scotland, incorporeal moveable property) such as goodwill, intellectual property, book debts and uncalled share capital or calls made but not paid. *Form 395* (see page 43) is used in registering a mortgage or charge and *Form 397* (see page 44) for an issue of secured debentures. Unless registered, the charge is void as against the liquidator and any creditor so far as any security on the company's assets is conferred under the charge and the moneys secured are immediately repayable. If incorrect particulars are registered, the charge is void to the extent of the irregularity unless the court orders otherwise but the Registrar will allow a late amendment to the registered particulars. The company and its officers who are in default in registering the instruments are, in addition, liable to a fine of £200 a day until registration is effected and the holder of the unregistered charge is in the position of an unsecured creditor.

A copy of the certificate of registration issued by the Registrar must be endorsed on every debenture or certificate of debenture stock issued by the company unless the charge was created after the issue.

Copies of every instrument creating a charge which requires registration must be kept at the registered office but it is only necessary to provide a copy of one of a series of uniform debentures.

Charges on registered land must also be registered under the Land

M

COMPANIES FORM No. 395

Particulars of a charge

Pursuant to section 395 of the Companies Act 1985

395

Please do not
write in
this margin

**Please complete
legibly, preferably
in black type, or
bold block lettering**

To the Registrar of Companies
(Address overleaf - Note 5)

For official use

Company number

* insert full name
of company

Name of company

*

Date of creation of the charge

Description of the instrument (if any) creating or evidencing the charge (note 2)

Amount secured by the charge

Names and addresses of the chargees or persons entitled to the charge

Postcode

Presentor's name address and
reference (if any):

For official Use
Mortgage Section

Post room

Page 1

Time critical reference

43

M

COMPANIES FORM No. 397

**Particulars for the registration
of a charge to secure a series
of debentures**

397

Please do not
write in
this margin

Pursuant to section 397 of the Companies Act 1985

Please complete
legibly, preferably
in black type, or
bold block lettering

To the Registrar of Companies
(Address overleaf - Note 6)

For official use

Company number

Name of company

* insert full
name of
company

*

Date of the covering deed (if any) (note 2) _____

Total amount secured by the whole series _____

Date of present issue _____

Amount of present issue (if any) of debentures of the series _____

Dates of resolutions authorising the issue of the series _____

Names of the trustees (if any) for the debenture holders

General description of the property charged

Continue overleaf as necessary

Presentor's name address and
reference (if any):

For official Use
Mortgage Section

Post room

Time critical Reference

Page 1

44

M

COMPANIES FORM No. 403a

Declaration of satisfaction in full or in part of mortgage or charge

403a

Pursuant to section 403(1) of the Companies Act 1985

Please do not
write in
this margin

**Please complete
legibly, preferably
in black type or,
bold block lettering**

To the Registrar of Companies
(Address overleaf)

For official use

Company number

Name of company

* insert full name
of company

```
*
```

I, _____

of _____

† delete as
appropriate

‡ insert a description
of the instrument(s)
creating or
evidencing the
charge, eg
'Mortgage',
'Charge',
'Debenture' etc.

ø the date of
registration may be
confirmed from the
certificate

§ insert brief
details of
property

[a director][the secretary][the administrator][the administrative receiver]† of the above company, do

solemnly and sincerely declare that the debt for which the charge described below was given has been

paid or satisfied in **[full][part]**†

Date and Description of charge‡ _____

Date of Registrationø _____

Name and address of [chargee][trustee for the debenture holders] _____

_____

Short particulars of property charged§ _____

_____

And I make this solemn declaration conscientiously believing the same to be true and by virtue of the

provisions of the Statutory Declarations Act 1835.

Declared at _____

_____

_____

the _____ day of _____

one thousand nine hundred and _____

before me _____

A Commissioner for Oaths or Notary Public or Justice of
the Peace or Solicitor having the powers conferred on a
Commissioner for Oaths

Declarant to sign below

Presentor's name address and
reference (if any):

For official Use	
Mortgage Section	Post room

45

Registration Act 1925, and fixed charges on unregistered land registered under the Land Charges Act 1972.

When a registered charge is repaid or satisfied a 'memorandum of satisfaction' on *Form 403a* (see page 45) should be filed with the Registrar.

The Consumer Credit Act

Loans for less than £15,000 including the cost of the credit, where the company is a joint debtor with an individual, must comply with the terms of the Consumer Credit Act 1974. A joint and several obligation by the company and an individual is outside the ambit of the Act.

◀ CHAPTER 4 ▶

DIRECTORS

The private limited company must have at least one director, although he cannot also be the secretary; your Articles can specify the maximum number of directors.

Who is a director?

Anyone, with whatever title and however appointed, who acts as a director, is regarded as a director.

Who can be a director?

Who is eligible?

Anyone can be appointed as director unless disqualified by the Articles except for:

- an undischarged bankrupt, unless his or her appointment is approved by the court;
- someone disqualified by court order;
- the company's auditor.

Your Articles usually disqualify anyone who is of unsound mind or who is absent from board meetings for more than six months without consent. A company can be your corporate director, and directors need not hold shares unless this is required by the Articles.

Appointment

Appointment of directors

The first directors can be appointed:

- by the subscribers to the Memorandum (who must sign the Notice of Appointment filed on incorporation) unless the Articles permit a majority to act;
- by naming them in the Articles, when the appointment takes effect from the date of incorporation;
- by appointment at the first company meeting;
- by appointment under a specific provision in the Articles.

Additional and subsequent appointments are made in accordance with the Articles and you can provide for appointment by shareholders in proportion to their holdings. The usual provision permits appointment by the board to fill vacancies, or to appoint additional directors subject to a specified maximum. The new director must then retire at the Annual General Meeting following appointment, immediately standing for re-election and, unless the Articles provide otherwise, the shareholders must have 28 days' notice of the proposal.

Details of the *appointment* of directors must be filed on *Form 288a*, signed by the officer confirming his consent to act but the appointment is effective even if the notice is not filed. The resignation or retirement of directors or the secretary and changes in their particulars, however, must be filed with the Registrar on *Forms 288a, 228b*, and *228c* respectively (see pages 49–51).

Retirement or
removal of
directors

Retirement and removal

Usually, a third of the directors retire by rotation each year, standing for re-election at the Annual General Meeting unless the Articles otherwise provide. They are technically out of office until re-elected by the shareholders.

Removal is by a majority vote of the shareholders and the shareholders and the director must have 28 days' notice of the proposal.

The board

The board of directors

The directors cannot act alone and must work through the board which

288a

APPOINTMENT of director or secretary

(NOT for resignation (use Form 288b) or change of particulars (use Form 288c))

COMPANIES HOUSE

Please complete in typescript, or in bold black capitals.

✳F 2 8 8 A 0 1 8 ✳

Company Number	
Company Name in full	

	Day	Month	Year		Day	Month	Year
Date of appointment				†Date of Birth			

Appointment form

Notes on completion appear on reverse.

Appointment as director ☐   as secretary ☐   *Please mark the appropriate box. If appointment is as a director and secretary mark both boxes.*

NAME

*Style / Title		*Honours etc	
Forename(s)			
Surname			
Previous Forename(s)		Previous Surname(s)	
Usual residential address			
Post town		Postcode	
County / Region		Country	
†Nationality		†Business occupation	
†Other directorships (additional space overleaf)			

I consent to act as ** director / secretary of the above named company

Consent signature		Date	

* Voluntary details.
† Directors only.

A director, secretary etc must sign the form below.

Signed		Date	

** Please delete as appropriate

(**a director / secretary / administrator / administrative receiver / receiver manager / receiver)

Please give the name, address, telephone number and, if available, a DX number and Exchange of the person Companies House should contact if there is any query.

	Tel
DX number	DX exchange

Companies House receipt date barcode

When you have completed and signed the form please send it to the Registrar of Companies at:

Companies House, Crown Way, Cardiff, CF4 3UZ   DX 33050 Cardiff
for companies registered in England and Wales   or
Companies House, 37 Castle Terrace, Edinburgh, EH1 2EB
for companies registered in Scotland   DX 235 Edinburgh

Form revised March 1995

COMPANIES HOUSE

Please complete in typescript,
or in bold black capitals.

288b

RESIGNATION of director or secretary
(*NOT for appointment (use Form 288a) or change of particulars (use Form 288c)*)

Company Number

Company Name in full

✱F 2 8 8 B 0 1 9 ✱

Resignation form

Date of resignation | Day | Month | Year

Resignation as director   as secretary   Please mark the appropriate box. If resignation is as a director and secretary mark both boxes.

NAME   *Style / Title   *Honours etc

Please insert details as previously notified to Companies House.

Forename(s)

Surname

†Date of Birth | Day | Month | Year

If cessation is other than resignation, please state reason

A serving director, secretary etc must sign the form below.

Signed   **Date**

* Voluntary details.
† Directors only.

(by a serving director / secretary / administrator / administrative receiver / receiver manager / receiver)

Please give the name, address, telephone number and, if available, a DX number and Exchange of the person Companies House should contact if there is any query.

Tel

DX number   DX exchange

Companies House receipt date barcode

When you have completed and signed the form please send it to the Registrar of Companies at:
Companies House, Crown Way, Cardiff, CF4 3UZ   **DX 33050 Cardiff**
for companies registered in England and Wales   **or**
Companies House, 37 Castle Terrace, Edinburgh, EH1 2EB
for companies registered in Scotland   **DX 235 Edinburgh**

Form revised March 1995

50

COMPANIES HOUSE

Please complete in typescript,
or in bold black capitals.

288c

CHANGE OF PARTICULARS for
director or secretary (*NOT for appointment*
(*use Form 288a*) or resignation (*use Form 288b*))

Company Number

Company Name in full

F288C01A

Changes of particulars form   *Complete in all cases*

	Day	Month	Year
Date of change of particulars			

Name   *Style / Title*   *Honours etc

Forename(s)

Surname

	Day	Month	Year
† Date of Birth			

Change of name (*enter new name*) Forename(s)

Surname

Change of usual residential address
(*enter new address*)

Post town

County / Region   Postcode

Country

Other change   (*please specify*)

A serving director, secretary etc must sign the form below.

Signed   **Date**

* Voluntary details.
† Directors only.

(by a serving director / secretary / administrator / administrative receiver / receiver manager / receiver)

Please give the name, address, telephone number and, if available, a DX number and Exchange of the person Companies House should contact if there is any query.

Tel

DX number   DX exchange

Companies House receipt date barcode

When you have completed and signed the form please send it to the Registrar of Companies at:
Companies House, Crown Way, Cardiff, CF4 3UZ   **DX 33050 Cardiff**
for companies registered in England and Wales   or
Companies House, 37 Castle Terrace, Edinburgh, EH1 2EB
for companies registered in Scotland   **DX 235 Edinburgh**

Form revised March 1995

51

usually conducts and controls company business. Formal meetings are, however, often dispensed with and the board can delegate its powers to one or more board members and appoint a managing director.

Part-time directors. Non-executive directors with financial, legal or technical expertise can be appointed.

Alternate directors who speak and act on behalf of board members in their temporary absence can be appointed if you have an appropriate provision in the Articles.

Nominee directors are appointed to represent substantial shareholders. They must not act solely in their principal's interests but, like any other director, in the interests of the company as a whole.

Shadow directors are persons in accordance with whose instructions the directors are accustomed to act and they have the same duties and obligations as any other directors. Your professional advisers, however, are not regarded as shadow directors.

Directors as employees

Directors are company employees; they have no right under the Articles to remuneration, notice or compensation for loss of office but they have the same rights as other employees under the employment legislation provided they receive a salary. They should therefore be employed under a service contract setting out their terms and conditions of employment, including pension arrangements, the level of contributions to be paid for life assurance and details of benefits in kind.

Contracts exceeding five years must be approved by the company in general meeting and must be available for inspection at the company's registered office or principal place of business. If there is no full written contract, a written memorandum or note of the terms of employment must be included and details of the place of inspection must be sent to the Registrar.

Directors' duties

A director is a constitutional monarch bound by the terms of the

Directors as employees

Duties

52

company's charter set out in the Memorandum and Articles. He can exercise all the powers permitted by them which are not reserved to be exercised by the shareholders in general meeting. If he is the majority shareholder and sole director, his rule may be despotic.

He must, however, act in accordance with the Companies Acts and the general law and he has three primary duties:

- a fiduciary duty to the company to act honestly and in good faith and in the best interests of the company as a whole;
- a duty to exercise such a degree of skill and care in carrying out his duties as might reasonably be expected from someone of his ability and experience;
- a duty to carry out the statutory obligations imposed by the Companies Acts and other legislation.

Fiduciary duty

Directors in position of trust

This is the duty to act honestly, in good faith and in the best interests of the company, which imposes a trustee's responsibility on directors to take proper care of the assets and to ensure payments are properly made and supported by adequate documentation. Directors must not make a personal profit at the company's expense and must disclose to the other directors at board meetings any interest in company transactions. Disclosure should also be made at general meetings and it should be formally minuted.

The directors' personal interests must not conflict with those of the company and they must not use its assets, including knowledge acquired through the company, for personal benefit.

Directors as agents

Directors as agents

Because the company is a separate legal person, a director can only act as the company's agent, acting on his principal's (the company's) instructions, express or implied. For instance, the director's signature on a company contract binds the company but if he signs contracts in his own name, without any reference to the company, he can be personally liable under the contract.

53

Interest in contracts

Company contracts

Directors' personal interests and the interests of persons connected with them (see page 56), direct or indirect, in company contracts must be disclosed. Disclosure must be to the board, and the director cannot thereafter take part in discussing the transaction. If the interested director votes on the contract the transaction can be set aside by the company. In some circumstances details must also be shown in the audited accounts (see pages 76–77).

Loans to directors, connected persons and employees

Borrowing from the company

Special Companies Acts provisions apply to loans and lending facilities extended to directors and their 'connections'.

There is no limit on the facility if the transaction is made in the ordinary course of the company's business and might properly have been made, on the same terms, to an outsider, or if the company is in the lending business. Nor is there a limit on the amount the company can provide to enable a director properly to perform his duties but the transaction must then be approved in advance by the shareholders in general meeting or made on condition that, if not approved at the next Annual General Meeting, the company will be reimbursed within six months of the meeting.

Money-lending companies

Money-lending companies which ordinarily provide such loans to employees can lend up to £100,000 to a director to buy, or pay for improvements to, his only or main residence for tax purposes. This is, however, a maximum from which must be deducted any other cash or credit facilities already extended to the director.

The money-lending company can also make loans or quasi-loans or extend guarantees to directors or their connections, provided that the company would give a similar facility to an outsider in the ordinary course of its business. For this purpose a quasi-loan is an undertaking by the company to reimburse a creditor of the director or connected person.

Loans, guarantees, security for loans and advances

A company can make a loan, extend a guarantee or provide security in connection with a loan to a director, shadow director or anyone 'connected with' them to a maximum of £5000.

The company can advance up to £20,000 to a director to enable him to meet properly incurred business expenses.

Connected persons

Persons 'connected with' a director broadly comprise the director's partner, spouse, child and step-child, a company with which the director is associated and of which he controls at least one-fifth of the votes at general meetings, a trustee of any trust under which the director, the family group or the associated companies are beneficiaries, and the partner of a 'connected' person.

Loans to employees

There is no top limit on an advance made to set up a trust to buy shares in the company for employees, including full-time salaried directors, or on the amount employees may borrow to buy company shares. The company can, however, assist anyone in the purchase of its shares, provided that the company's assets are not thereby reduced or, to the extent of the reduction, the finance comes out of distributable profits.

The assistance can be by gift, loan guarantee, security, indemnity or any other financial help which materially reduces the net assets.

The smaller business has some tax concessions here but the statutory provisions are complicated and you should seek expert advice before calling on your company's generosity.

The Consumer Credit Act 1974

Transactions of under £15,000, including the cost of the credit, must comply with the terms of the Consumer Credit Act 1974.

Use of company assets

Private use of company assets is restricted. Non-cash assets valued at £2000, or at an amount equal to the company's paid-up share capital,

Private use of
company assets

cannot be acquired by the company or handed over to directors or connected persons without the prior approval of the shareholders in general meeting. Approval can be retrospective if given within a reasonable period of the transaction. If annual accounts have been prepared in accordance with the Companies Acts, the limit goes up to £100,000 or a maximum of 10 per cent of the company's net assets as stated in the most recent accounts.

Disclosure

Credit facilities, agreements to arrange credit, and the provision of guarantees and security to directors and connected persons must be disclosed in the annual accounts or the directors' report, unless the company's contingent net liability during the period covered by the accounts does not exceed £5000. Any other transactions or arrangements between the directors and connected persons must also be included in the accounts, unless the net value does not exceed £1000 or 1 per cent of the net value of the company's assets to a maximum of £5000.

Penalties for contravening legislation

Fines and penalties

Credit facilities extended in contravention of the legislation and *ultra vires* transactions can be cancelled by the company, which is entitled to reimbursement unless this is impossible, or the company has been indemnified for loss and damage, or an outsider without knowledge of the contravention might suffer loss. If restitution is not possible, the contravenor and any director authorising the transaction are liable to reimburse or indemnify the company and, in addition, to recompense it for any consequential gain or loss unless they can prove they did not know the transaction was unlawful. If the transaction is with a director's connection, the connected director is not liable if he took all reasonable steps to ensure that the company complied with the Companies Acts.

There is no way to save an unlawful transfer of assets by providing an indemnity through a third party.

Share dealings

There is no restriction on directors' share and debenture dealings, as long as the company is kept informed and details entered on the company's Register of Directors' Interests.

Skill and care

Directors must exercise the degree of skill and care that may reasonably be expected from someone in their position with their ability and experience. Professionally qualified directors must therefore act with the care and diligence expected from a member of their profession and, unless they are part-time directors, should devote themselves full time to the job.

Non-executive directors are usually not involved in day-to-day management and the only requirement is that they regularly attend board meetings, but they must exercise an independent standard of judgement and if they are properly to fulfil the purpose of their appointment they should be encouraged to participate fully in board decisions.

Delegation

The directors can delegate their duties but they must be satisfied that they are delegating to a suitable person who is competent, reliable and honest. They cannot simply abandon responsibility but must keep themselves informed as to progress.

Statutory duties

The directors' **administrative duties** are contained mainly in the Companies Acts and the Insolvency Act 1986.

Both the company and its officers can be fined for failure to comply with the statutory requirements, and persistent default can lead to disqualification from acting as a director or from being involved in company management for up to 15 years, or imprisonment. Fines, payable on demand, apply to the late filing of accounts. They range from £100 for accounts delivered up to three months late to £1000 for a delay of over 12 months and are in addition to fines imposed on the directors in the criminal courts. The criminal penalties for failure to deliver the accounts or the annual return and failure to notify a change of directors or company secretary are set out in Appendix 3. Directors of small companies therefore often pass these duties to their accountants or solicitors (who are experienced in company administration) so that they can concentrate on management. This is an appropriate delegation of duty but the directors are still required to supervise and they are ultimately responsible for ensuring that the company complies with legal requirements.

The **statutory books** and the **annual return** are dealt with on pages 65 and 66. Although the company secretary is responsible for maintaining the statutory books, the directors' duty to supervise requires that they ensure the company keeps proper records and files the necessary documentation with the Registrar in compliance with the statutory requirements.

Directors' liability

Directors' liability

Limited liability means that the company is responsible for business debts and obligations. Liabilities can, however, be passed to directors and management but only in specific circumstances.

The directors have unlimited power to bind the company, whatever the restrictions imposed by the Memorandum, the Articles or the shareholders, provided the person with whom they are dealing is acting in good faith. However, the company can repudiate an *ultra vires* transaction entered into by a director, a connected person or the board. The directors or the board may then be liable to the company but a connected person is only liable if he knew that the directors were exceeding their powers.

The directors are liable personally for breach of statutory or other duty or where there is fraud but they are only liable for negligence if they are clearly at fault.

Directors may also be liable personally if they, or the company, to their knowledge act outside the powers given by the Memorandum and Articles or if they contract without reference to the company by, for instance, placing orders without stating that they are acting on behalf of the company. They are also liable on cheques and other negotiable instruments which do not carry the company's full registered name.

Directors are liable for 'misfeasance' (wrongdoing): for instance making secret profits at the company's expense. 'Nonfeasance' (doing nothing), however, may bring no liability unless it comes within the matters to be considered on an application for disqualification; a director can apply to the court for relief in any proceedings for negligence, default, breach of duty or breach of trust and the court will relieve him of liability if satisfied that he acted reasonably and honestly and, in the circumstances, ought fairly to be excused.

Employers' duties

The legal obligations imposed on employers relating to employees and third parties affected by the company's business activities apply to all employers. Because of the protection of limited liability, claims are made against the company; although the directors are responsible for ensuring compliance with the law, liability is only passed to them if there is fraud or, in some circumstances, negligence.

The directors, the company and the shareholders

Minority shareholders have no say in the running of the business and if management is inefficient a shareholder may be able to do nothing. It is only the company itself – that is, the majority shareholders – who can take action, and provided directors act in good faith and in the interests of the company as a whole, the majority shareholders can do anything permitted by the Memorandum and Articles and can ratify almost any transaction, even retrospectively, in general meeting.

A single shareholder can, however, sue the company in his own name to protect his individual rights, for example to compel the board to accept his vote at general meetings or if there is unfair prejudice, fraud or 'gross negligence'. A group of 10 per cent of the shareholders can call in the Department of Trade and Industry to investigate the company and in some circumstances the court can take action against management. The directors may then lose the protection of limited liability and be ordered to compensate the company or the shareholder for loss.

Directors and outsiders

Third party claims on directors are usually made by unpaid creditors when the company goes into insolvent liquidation and the protection of limited liability is lost if there has been fraudulent or wrongful trading. Liability can fall on non-executive shadow and nominee directors, as well as full-time working directors.

Fraudulent trading is trading with intent to defraud creditors and can arise when cheques are paid into the company's bank account after a company stops trading, even if paid in under the genuine and reasonable belief that creditors will be paid in a short time. Floating charges and loans are invalid if made within six months of a winding up, unless the company was solvent when the loan was made; in some circumstances the directors must repay the creditor and may also be liable to prosecution.

Wrongful trading. Penalties here extend to disqualification and imprisonment but only if it is proved that at some time before the liquidation the company was trading although the director knew, or ought to have known, that there was no reasonable prospect that it could avoid insolvent liquidation.

For 12 months after insolvent liquidation the directors and shadow directors cannot act for a company with the same name. The court's consent is required before they act for a company using its former name or trading name or one suggesting a continuing association with it.

Personal guarantees become a problem only when the company cannot pay its debts and a guarantee on the bank overdraft is probably the most usual undertaking required from directors in support of a company, often backed up by a charge on a director's home. The bank usually requires the director's spouse to be a joint and several guarantor, as this gives the bank priority to the spouse's claim to the equity in the property. A director is advised to resist a request for a charge on personal assets, particularly on his home, as a charge given for business purposes removes the protection under the general law given to residential owners, and independent legal advice should be sought before any guarantees are given.

Leases

Business leases

Landlords often require directors to join in a lease of company premises as surety. If the company cannot pay rent, the landlord can then turn to the directors for payment and they remain liable until the lease expires, even if the lease is assigned or the landlord consents to their release.

Commercial contracts

Finance companies often require directors to guarantee payments made by the company on instalment contracts. The contracts provide that in the event of premature termination, the full balance is immediately due and payable, and the directors are liable to pay the full amount if the company cannot do so.

Insurance

The 1989 Companies Act permits the company to indemnify its officers and auditors against liability for negligence, default, breach of duty and breach of trust. The cover is for both civil and criminal proceedings, provided judgment is given in their favour, they are acquitted or relief is granted by the court. You may want to arrange additional insurance to cover the unindemnifiable risk, with the party at risk paying an appropriate proportion of the premium.

The Articles must, however, include an appropriate provision giving the company the power to purchase the insurance, and details of the insurance must be included in the directors' report.

Disqualification

Directors may be disqualified:

Disqualification of directors

- on conviction for an offence connected with the promotion, formation, management or liquidation of the company;
- in a winding up, if the company continued to trade with intent to defraud creditors;
- if guilty of a fraud in relation to the company;
- for non-compliance with the Companies Acts, but there must have been 'persistent default', that is, at least three offences within five years.

Disqualification can be for up to 15 years and the court has discretion whether or not to make the order. It must, however, disqualify a director whose conduct in relation to the company, alone or together with his conduct as director of another company, makes him, in the court's opinion, unfit to be concerned in the management of a company.

The *Register of Disqualification Orders*, maintained by the Secretary of State, is open to public inspection; anyone acting while disqualified is jointly and severally liable with the company employing him for debts incurred during the period of disqualification, and liability extends to anyone acting on their instructions.

The Companies House disqualified directors list gives details of disqualification orders for directors in England, Wales and Scotland. It is on microfiche and is updated weekly.

◄ CHAPTER 5 ►

RUNNING THE COMPANY

The price of limited liability is a certain amount of publicity – documentation and reports must be sent to the Companies Registry, where some are available for public inspection on payment of a fee. In addition, you must make regular reports to shareholders and accounts must conform with the requirements of the Companies Acts.

The registered office

Your company must have a registered office to which formal communications and notices, including notice of legal proceedings, are sent. The address determines the tax district which deals with the company's return and tax affairs, except for PAYE which is usually dealt with by the local collector of taxes where the wages records are kept.

The address need not be the company's main trading address and it is often convenient to use the address of the company's accountant or solicitor.

Registered office and trading address

Displaying the company name

The company name must be fixed to, or painted on, the outside of the registered office in a prominent position, as well as at each of the company's offices, factories and places of business.

Display of company name

Business letters and other documentation

The company name must appear on all business letters, cheques and other negotiable instruments, order forms, invoices and on the company seal. The letterhead must also show the registered number and registered office address but you can choose to list the names either of all directors or none of them – you cannot list a selection of named directors.

If the company is registered for VAT, invoices must in addition show the VAT registration number, the invoice number, date of supply, description of the supply, amount payable excluding VAT, the rate of VAT and the amount, the rate of any cash discount and the customer's name and address.

Directors

The appointment and removal of directors and their obligations are dealt with in Chapter 4 and you may want to appoint a **managing director**, although he has no specific powers under the Companies Acts. His authority is based entirely on the terms and conditions of his service contract or those imposed by the board.

Table A enables the directors to delegate any of their powers to the managing director, who often looks after day-to-day management although he will not usually exercise the company's borrowing powers.

The chairman is the director who chairs board and general meetings. He can be named in the Articles, be appointed at the first directors' meeting to hold office for a specified period, or be appointed at each meeting to act as chairman. Table A gives him a casting vote if there is deadlock on the board and he has no other special powers although they can be set out in the Articles.

Company secretary

The company must have a company secretary, who can also be a director provided he is not the sole director. The secretary has important duties and obligations; Table A provides that he be appointed by the directors for such term at such remuneration and on such conditions as they may think fit and they can also remove him.

The secretary is the company's chief administrative officer with ostensible authority in day-to-day administrative matters. His duties include the convening of board and company meetings, taking minutes of meetings, keeping the company's statutory books up to date, filing returns and forms with the Registrar and dealing with share transfers and proxies.

The first secretary must be named in the documents lodged prior to registration so his appointment should be minuted at the first directors' meeting.

The statutory books

The company secretary is responsible for maintaining the statutory registers and books. The statutory requirements are technical and in many smaller companies they are kept by the auditors, who also file the necessary documentation with the Registrar.

The statutory books are a useful record of the company's business activities and comprise:

The **Register of Members**, which lists the names and addresses of the subscribers to the Memorandum of Association and of all other shareholders, with details of their shareholdings. It must be kept at the registered office or at some other office designated by the directors. Entries can be removed after a person has ceased to hold shares for 20 years.

The **Register of Debenture Holders**, which lists similar information relating to debenture holders.

The **Register of Directors and Secretaries**, setting out the directors' full forenames and surnames and any former names, their usual residential address, nationality, business occupation and details of any other directorships held within the previous five years. The secretary needs to provide only his present and former forenames and surnames and his residential address.

The **Register of Directors' Interests**, listing directors' holdings. This must include details of rights given to subscribe for shares or debentures, specifying the period during which they may be exercised and the consideration in cash or asset value; further information must be entered when the rights are exercised.

The **Register of Charges** with details of mortgages and fixed and floating charges secured on the company's assets, consisting of a short description of the property charged, the amount of the charge and the names of the lenders, except in the case of securities to bearer.

The **Minute Book**. Proceedings at general meetings and directors' meetings must be recorded in minute books; when duly signed by the chairman, they are evidence of the proceedings.

The statutory books can be bound or looseleaf but precautions should be taken against falsification. They must be kept at the registered office or other place of business designated by the directors and available for inspection by shareholders without charge for at least two hours a day and copies must be provided on payment of a fee. Creditors as well as shareholders are entitled to inspect copies of the instruments creating registrable charges and the register without charge and they can also be inspected by outsiders on payment of a fee. Access to minutes of directors' meetings is available only to the directors, the secretary and the auditors and the office may be closed and the books inaccessible for up to 30 days, provided you advertise the closure. A full list of the books, registers and documents which must be available for inspection is set out in Appendix 4.

Annual return

Each year an annual return must be filed with the Registrar on *Form 363a* (see page 68). The return is made up to the 'return date', which is the anniversary of incorporation or, if the last return was made on a different date, on the anniversary of that date. The return basically summarises some of the information in the statutory books and changes during the year, including details of issued shares, a list of past and present shareholders, and details of directors and shadow directors (including their dates of birth) and of the secretary. Appointment of new directors, however, must be filed on *Form 288a* and the resignation or retirement of directors or the secretary and changes in their particulars on *Forms 288b* and *288c* respectively. A change in the registered office address must be filed on *Form 287*.

The classification scheme giving a company's 'type' is the same as that used for VAT trade classification, with the addition of three extra codes. Copies of VAT trade classifications are available from your local VAT enquiry office free of charge.

A copy of the annual return signed by a director or the secretary must be sent to the Registrar, with the registration fee of £18, within 28 days of the return date (see previous page).

If an annual return is not filed the company and the directors are liable to fines (see page 57).

The accounts

Accounts and accounting records

Accounting reference date

For companies incorporated after 1 April 1996 the date to which it will make up accounts each year is the last day of the month in which the anniversary of incorporation falls plus or minus seven days. For instance, your company incorporated on 16 October 1995 would have an ARD of 31 October and its accounts would cover the period from 16 October 1996 to 31 October 1997, plus or minus seven days. Notification of the date is sent to the Registrar on *Form 224* (see page 74). Accounts filed with a made-up date other than the ARD will be rejected by the Registrar and the company and directors will be liable to the fines set out on page 57.

The first accounting reference period starts on incorporation. Subsequent periods begin after the end of the previous period and are for 12 months unless the date is changed on application to the Registrar on Form 225 (see page 98) during the accounting year or during the period allowed for delivery of the accounts to the Registrar.

Accounting records

The Companies Acts require companies to keep accounting records to show and explain company transactions and reflect the company's financial position with reasonable accuracy. The directors are responsible for ensuring that the balance sheet and profit and loss accounts are set out in the form prescribed in the Acts and that they give a 'true and fair view' of the company's financial position and its transactions.

Crown copyright. Reproduced with the permission of the Controller of Her Majesty's Stationery Office.

Please complete in typescript, or in bold black capitals.

363a

Annual Return

Company Number [   ]

Company Name in full [   ]

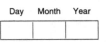

F363A012

Date of this return *(See note 1)*
The information in this return is made up to

Day	Month	Year

Date of next return *(See note 2)*
If you wish to make your next return to a date earlier than the anniversary of this return please show the date here. Companies House will then send a form at the appropriate time.

Day	Month	Year

Registered Office *(See note 3)*
Show here the address **at the date of this return.**

Any change of registered office **must** *be notified on form 287.*

Post town

County / Region

Postcode

Principal business activities
(See note 4)
Show trade classification code number(s) for the principal activity or activities.

If the code number cannot be determined, give a brief description of principal activity.

When you have completed and signed the form please send it to the Registrar of Companies at:

Companies House, Crown Way, Cardiff, CF4 3UZ   DX 33050 Cardiff
for companies registered in England and Wales
or
Companies House, 37 Castle Terrace, Edinburgh, EH1 2EB
for companies registered in Scotland   **DX 235 Edinburgh**

Form revised March 1995

Page 1

Register of members *(See note 5)*

If the register of members is not kept at the registered office, state here where it is kept.

Post town

County / Region   Postcode

Register of Debenture holders

(See note 6)

If there is a register of debenture holders and it is not kept at the registered office, state here where it is kept.

Post town

County / Region   Postcode

Company type *(See note 7)*

Public limited company

Private company limited by shares

Private company limited by guarantee without share capital

Private company limited by shares exempt under section 30

Private company limited by guarantee exempt under section 30

Private unlimited company with share capital

Private unlimited company without share capital

> Please mark the appropriate box

Company Secretary *(see notes 1-5)*

Details of a new company secretary must be notified on form 288a.

(Please photocopy this area to provide details of joint secretaries).

Name   * Style / Title   *Honours etc

Forename(s)

Surname

* Voluntary details.

Previous forename(s)

Previous surname(s)

Address

Usual residential address must be given. In the case of a corporation, give the registered or principal office address.

Post town

County / Region   Postcode

Country

Page 2

69

Directors (see notes 1-5)

Please list directors in alphabetical order.

Details of new directors must be notified on form 288a

Name   * Style / Title

* Honours etc

Forename(s)

Surname

Previous forename(s)

Previous surname(s)

Day   Month   Year

Date of birth

Address

*Usual residential
address* must be
given. In the case of a
corporation, give the
registered or principal
office address.

Post town

County / Region   Postcode

Country   **Nationality**

Business occupation

Other directorships

* Voluntary details.

Name   * Style / Title

* Honours etc

Forename(s)

Surname

Previous forename(s)

Previous surname(s)

Day   Month   Year

Date of birth

Address

*Usual residential
address* must be
given. In the case of a
corporation, give the
registered or principal
office address.

Post town

County / Region   Postcode

Country   **Nationality**

Business occupation

Other directorships

Issued share capital (see note 9)
Enter details of all the shares in issue at the date of this return.

Class (e.g. Ordinary/Preference)	Number of shares issued	Aggregate Nominal Value (i.e Number of shares issued multiplied by nominal value per share)
Totals		

List of past and present members
(Use attached schedule where appropriate)
A full list is required if one was not included with either of the last two returns.
(see note 10)

There were no changes in the period ☐

               on paper   in another format

A list of changes is enclosed ☐ ☐

A full list of members is enclosed ☐ ☐

Elective resolutions
(Private companies only)
(See note 11)

If at the date of this return an election is in force to dispense with annual general meetings, *mark this box* ☐

If at the date of this return an election is in force to dispense with laying accounts in general meetings, *mark this box* ☐

Certificate

I certify that the information given in this return is true to the best of my knowledge and belief.

Signed [_____] **Date** [_____]

† Please delete as appropriate.

† a director /secretary

When you have signed the return send it with the fee to the Registrar of Companies. Cheques should be made payable to **Companies House.**

This return includes [_____] continuation sheets.
(enter number)

Please give the name, address, telephone number, and if available, a DX number and Exchange, for the person Companies House should contact if there is any query.

Tel
DX number   DX exchange

**Pages 5 and 6 of
Form 363a
replicate page 3**

COMPANIES HOUSE

*Please complete in typescript,
or in bold black capitals.*

Crown copyright.
Reproduced with
the permission of
the Controller of
Her Majesty's
Stationery Office.

List of past and present members
Schedule to form 363a, 363b

Company Number	
Company Name in full	

	Number of shares or amount of stock held by existing members at date of this return.	Particulars of shares or stock transferred since the date of the last return (or in the case of the first return, since the incorporation of the company) by (a) persons who are still members, and (b) persons who have ceased to be members.		
Name and address	Number or amount currently held	Number or amount Transferred	Date of registration of transfer	Remarks

Records must be maintained on a day-to-day basis to include:

- details of cash receipts and payments on a daily basis, including details of the transactions to which they relate;
- a list of assets and liabilities;
- a statement of stock of goods held at the end of (each) financial year with details of stock takings on which the records are based;
- with the exception of retailers, a sufficient description of goods and services bought and sold to enable sellers and purchasers to be identified.

Records must be retained for at least three years, but if you are registered for VAT they must be retained for a minimum of six years.

The company's accounts

Copies of the company's accounts, comprising the balance sheet, approved by the board and signed on their behalf by a director, the profit and loss account, the auditor's report and the directors' report, approved by the board and signed on their behalf by a director or the secretary, must, unless the company has elected to dispense with this requirement, (see page 85) be put before the shareholders in general meeting within ten months of the end of the accounting reference period. Twenty-one days before the meeting copies must be sent to all share and debenture holders and to anyone else entitled to be given notice of the meeting, such as the auditors, and copies must be sent to the Registrar. Share and debenture holders are also entitled to receive a free copy of the company's last accounts.

The directors are liable to fines for delay in filing the accounts with the Registrar, depending on the length of the delay (see page 57). There is, however, no requirement to lay the accounts before the shareholders or agree them with the Inland Revenue before they are filed.

The accounts must be in English but can be in Welsh if you trade in Wales, when an English translation must be annexed to the accounts sent to the Registrar.

The new audit exemption

Small companies with a turnover that does not exceed £350,000 and with a balance sheet total of not more than £1.4m, can file unaudited

Exemption from audit for certain small companies

G

COMPANIES FORM No. 224

Notice of accounting reference date
(to be delivered within 9 months of incorporation)

224

Please do not write in this margin

Pursuant to section 224 of the Companies Act 1985 as inserted by section 3 of the Companies Act 1989

Please complete legibly, preferably in black type, or bold block lettering

To the Registrar of Companies **(Address overleaf)**

Company number

Name of company

*

* insert full name of company

gives notice that the date on which the company's accounting reference period is to be treated as coming to an end in each successive year is as shown below:

Important
The accounting reference date to be entered alongside should be completed as in the following examples:

Day   Month

5 April
Day   Month

| 0 | 5 | 0 | 4 |

30 June
Day   Month

| 3 | 0 | 0 | 6 |

31 December
Day   Month

| 3 | 1 | 1 | 2 |

‡ Insert Director, Secretary, Administrator, Administrative Receiver or Receiver (Scotland) as appropriate

Signed   Designation‡   Date

Presentor's name address telephone number and reference (if any):

For official use
D.E.B.   Post room

accounts. Although full accounts can be filed, the requirement is only for an abbreviated balance sheet with explanatory notes. Shareholders are, however, entitled to see the profit and loss account and the directors' report. Exemption from audit can be claimed for earlier years if the accounts were approved by the board on or after 11 August 1994 and delivered on time; if delivered late they must be accompanied by an auditor's report.

The balance sheet must include a statement by the directors referring to the relevant sections of the 1985 Act stating that:

- the company was entitled to the exemption
- shareholders have not deposited a notice requiring an audit
- the directors acknowledge their responsibility for
  i. ensuring the company keeps accounting records in compliance with the Companies Act 1985 and
  ii. preparing accounts giving a true and fair view of the company's affairs
- advantage has been taken of the various exemptions – details must be listed for individual accounts
- in the directors' opinion the company is entitled to take advantage of the exemption(s).

Shareholders with at least 10 per cent of the company's issued capital or at least 10 per cent of any class of shares are entitled to ask for an audit on giving written notice to the company's registered office at least one month before the end of the financial year.

Shareholders' entitlement to ask for an audit

If turnover exceeds £90,000 but is less than £350,000, the unaudited account must be accompanied by an accountant's report. This must state whether the accounts agree with the company's accounting records, whether they have been drawn up in compliance with the Companies Act 1985 as amended and whether the company is entitled to the exemption from audit.

NB Your Articles should be checked to ensure that you are not precluded from taking advantage of the audit exemptions.

The 'exemption for individual accounts'
The 'small' company, defined as one with a turnover that does not

exceed £2.8m, and/or whose balance sheet total is not more than £1.4m, and/or which employs fewer than 51 people may file abbreviated accounts with the Registrar. Fulfilment of two out of three of the criteria is sufficient to categorise the company. The abbreviated accounts include a modified balance sheet, although full accounts must still be sent to share and debenture holders. The modified balance sheet must contain a statement by the directors, immediately above their signatures, that they have relied on the exemption for individual accounts on the ground that the company is entitled to the benefit of them as a small company. A special auditors' report must also be filed, stating that in the auditors' opinion the requirements for exemption are satisfied, and their report must reproduce the full text of the auditors' report delivered to shareholders at the Annual General Meeting and annexed to the accounts circulated to shareholders.

The abbreviated accounts are an abbreviated version of the full balance sheet and aggregate amounts can be given for each item except for the figures relating to debtors and creditors. The debtors must be analysed to show separately for each item the amounts falling due after one year and creditors to show amounts falling due within one year and after one year. The information required where the directors' total remuneration is at least £60,000 need not be set out, nor need there be a statement (as is required on the full accounts) that they have been prepared in accordance with applicable accounting standards. Accounting policies adopted by the company, details of share capital and debentures, particulars of allotments and the basis of conversion of foreign currency amounts into sterling must be included and, where appropriate, comparative details and figures must be given for the previous financial year.

Contents of the accounts

The smaller company must include the following in the accounts:

- The aggregate amount of directors' and shadow directors' emoluments (ie salaries, fees, commission payments, expenses, pension contributions and the estimated money value of benefits received in kind). If the total is £60,000 or more, the accounts must instead set out the chairman's remuneration, amounts received by directors paid more than the chairman and state the number of directors paid less than £5000 and how many receive payments between successive multiples of £5000. Details of total payments waived by directors and payments and benefits received from third parties must also be included.

- Details of loans, credit arrangements and agreements for loans and credit arrangements made by the company with the directors and shadow directors and of any company transactions in which they have a direct or indirect material interest. ('Material' interests are not material if a majority of the directors – other than the interested party – thinks they are not material.)
- Details of transactions with persons connected with directors and shadow directors. A 'connected' person is the partner, spouse, child or step–child of a director or shadow director, a company with which the director or shadow director is associated and of which he controls at least one-fifth of the voting shares, a trustee of a trust under which the director, shadow director or connected person is a beneficiary, and the partner of a connected person. Details of credit transactions, guarantees and securities given for credit arrangements which involve amounts up to £5000 need not be included but credit facilities extended to company officers (excluding the directors) involving a total liability of £2500 must be set out.
- Details of directors' share and debenture holdings, and of subscription rights granted to or exercised by, the directors and their immediate family, although these can instead be included in the directors' report.

The directors' report, approved by the board and signed by a director or the secretary, need not be filed with the small company's accounts but the directors must report to shareholders. Their report must give a fair review of the development of business during the financial year and of the position at the year end, and state the amount recommended as dividend and the amount, if any, that the directors propose to carry to reserve or retain for investment.

In addition, the report must name the directors and state the company's principal activities and any change in the activities during the year. Significant changes in the fixed assets must be listed, as well as details of directors' interests in shares or debentures at the beginning and end of the year. Details must also be given of any important events affecting the company business and of research and development. Certain details of share transactions, employee training and welfare, and political and charitable contributions must also be specified.

The auditors are required to review the report, so you should ask them for assistance in ensuring that everything that materially affects the company's affairs is included.

Disclosing the accounts

The company's accounting records must be kept at the registered office or another office designated by the directors and be open to inspection by the company's officers at all times.

It is an offence to mislead the auditors and they are entitled to access to all the necessary documents and information in the preparation of the accounts.

Auditors

Auditors

The auditors can be appointed before the first general meeting at which the accounts are to be presented. They stay in office until the end of that meeting unless removed by ordinary (majority) vote of the shareholders. They must be appointed or re-appointed at every Annual General Meeting (AGM) for a term running from the conclusion of the meeting before which the accounts are laid until the end of the next AGM.

If for any reason the company is without an auditor, the directors or the company in general meeting can appoint a temporary replacement. If one is not appointed by the meeting the company must notify the Secretary of State within seven days of the meeting, when the Secretary of State may make the appointment.

The auditors must be members of the Institute of Chartered Accountants in England and Wales, Scotland or Ireland or of the Chartered Association of Certified Accountants. A director or employee cannot be the company's auditor but the auditor can act as the company's accountant, preparing company accounts and VAT and PAYE returns and generally giving secretarial assistance and taxation advice.

Responsibility for the proper administration of company affairs, however, rests with the directors. The auditors' only responsibility is for any loss caused by their own negligence or fraud. Their reports and conclusions must be based on proper investigation and they are entitled to access to all necessary documents and information. If they are not satisfied that your books and accounts properly reflect the company's financial circumstances, this must be stated in their report.

The company seal

Companies need no longer have a company seal which under earlier legislation was required to be used as the company's 'signature' and impressed on documents which had to be made deed. These include the company's commercial contracts, leases, share certificates, debentures and mortgages.

Until the 1989 Act dispensed with the requirement, the seal was the company's signature and the standard Articles required use of a seal – usually a metal disc with the full name of the company on it in raised letters. If the company must have a seal, its use must be authorised by the directors and usually the Articles provide that the affixing of the seal must be evidenced by the signature of a director and the company secretary.

However, under the 1989 Companies Act the signature of two directors, or a director and the company secretary, signing for and on behalf of the company now has the same effect as if the document had been executed (signed) under seal and your standard Articles can be changed (see pages 84 and 99) to take the provisions into account.

One problem remains at present: currently the only evidence of title to a share certificate is a certificate executed under seal. It is, however, proposed that share certificates be abolished so that title can be transferred via computer accounts.

Share issues

The directors must ensure that the Articles are complied with on share issues. The secretary records the issue of shares in the minutes of the meeting at which they are issued, and makes the appropriate entries in the Register of members to show the new shareholders' names and addresses and details of the shares issued.

Entries in the minutes and Register must also be made when shares are transferred.

Share certificates

The secretary completes share certificates which are numbered and state the number and class of shares issued. The certificate is signed by a director and the secretary and, if required by the Articles, sealed with the company seal. The same procedure applies to share transfers, except that the transfer form should be checked by the secretary to ensure that the correct stamp duty based on payment made for the shares has been paid to the Revenue and that it is stamped with the appropriate fee stamp.

Meetings

The method of calling and running meetings is set out in the Articles but procedure is more closely regulated for full company/shareholders' meetings than for directors' meetings, which can be run in any way that the directors think fit.

Single-member companies

The single-member company must, like any other company, have at least one director and a secretary who cannot also be the sole director. However, notwithstanding anything in the Articles to the contrary, the single member, present in person or by proxy, constitutes a quorum for meetings. A single-member 'shareholders' meeting' must be minuted as such and decisions must be formally notified to the company in writing, unless made by way of a written resolution.

If a contract between the company and a single shareholder who is also a director is not in writing, the terms of the contract must, unless the contract is made in the ordinary course of the company's business, be set out in a memorandum or recorded in the minutes of the next directors' meeting.

The 1989 Companies Act has simplified procedures for private companies and the relevant provisions are set out on page 84. They substantially reduce administration and costs and are particularly useful if there is a major overlap between ownership and management.

The following paragraphs apply, however, if you do not choose to take advantage of the new provisions.

The first board meeting

No notice is prescribed for calling board meetings; provided all the directors are notified they can decide to dispense with meetings, conducting business by telephone or correspondence. Table A includes a provision enabling written resolutions signed by all the directors to be as valid and effective as those passed at a duly convened and held meeting of directors. Otherwise, oral notice is sufficient and if a meeting is called a majority of the directors must attend; if a quorum is required by the Articles, the specified number of directors must be present.

The company exists from the date the Registrar issues the Certificate of Incorporation but a great deal of important company business cannot be dealt with until the first board meeting and it should therefore be held on the same day as, or as soon as possible after, incorporation.

Business will include:

- a report on the incorporation of the company, and the Certificate of Incorporation should be produced;
- reporting the appointment of the first directors and secretary;
- appointing the chairman;
- appointing any additional directors;
- reporting on the situation of the registered office and deciding whether it should be changed;
- adopting the company seal and confirming the authorised users and signatories;
- agreeing the opening of the **bank account** and naming the signatories, for instance any two directors or a director and the secretary. Your bank will provide a form of company mandate (agreement) which sets out the necessary wording. This must be sent to them with a copy of the Memorandum and Articles of Association and they will want to see the Certificate of Incorporation;
- the allotment of shares (other than the subscribers' shares) and a record of receipts of any payment received for the subscribers' shares and for any other shares allotted. Sealing of share certificates must be minuted;
- appointing the auditors and deciding on the accounting reference date.

You may also want to appoint a managing director or chairman, appoint solicitors, deal with matters relating to the company's trading activities and with general administrative matters, and disclose the directors' interests in contracts.

The meeting must be minuted by the secretary but minutes of directors'/board meetings are not available for shareholders' inspection; they should therefore be kept in a Minute Book separate from that used for minutes of company (shareholders') meetings.

General meetings

The shareholders acting together in general meeting can do anything *intra vires* (within the powers of) the company as set out in its Memorandum and Articles of Association. In practice, their power to control the company is delegated to the directors and exercised by resolutions passed in general meeting.

The secretary must keep minutes of meetings in the Minute Book kept for that purpose and when signed by the chairman of the meeting or the next successive meeting, they are evidence of the proceedings.

Voting

The Articles usually provide that voting is by a show of hands; each member, regardless of his shareholding, then has one vote. The Articles also usually provide that the chairman, or any two members, or a member or members holding not less than one-tenth of the total voting rights, can demand a poll when voting is normally on the basis of one vote per share held. Special voting rights attached to shares are taken into account before deciding whether a motion has been carried on a poll, and usually a proxy (authorised by an absent shareholder to vote on his behalf) can only vote on a poll.

A director's personal interest in a company contract disqualifies him from voting; if he does, the transaction can be set aside.

The Annual General Meeting

This must be held within 18 months of incorporation and once in every subsequent calendar year, 15 months being the longest permitted interval between meetings.

The meeting is more formal than a board meeting and motions must be proposed, seconded and voted on. The main business comprises:

- receiving the accounts and the directors' report;
- proposing the dividend;
- electing directors and re-electing those who retire by rotation;
- appointing or re-electing auditors and fixing their remuneration.

The holders of at least one-twentieth of the voting shares can force the company to present a resolution at the Annual General Meeting and to send their comments about it to all the shareholders. In exceptional circumstances a single director or shareholder can ask the court to order a meeting.

Extraordinary General Meetings

Any other company business is usually 'special' and requires an Extraordinary General Meeting, with notice to shareholders of what is to be discussed. The meeting is usually convened by the secretary, on the directors' instructions, to deal with business that cannot await the next Annual General Meeting.

Subject to the Articles, two or more holders of more than one-tenth of the fully paid-up voting shares can demand that the directors call a meeting within 21 days. In default, a meeting can be called by at least half of those shareholders within three months of the request.

Notice of meetings

Notice of meetings and of what is to be discussed must be given to shareholders and to the auditors in accordance with the provisions of the Articles. They usually specify 21 days for the Annual General Meeting and for meetings called to consider a special resolution, and 14 days for other meetings.

You must give 28 days' notice of a resolution to appoint new auditors or prevent their re-appointment and to remove or replace directors. Notice

Extraordinary General Meetings

Notices

83

of the resolution must be given at least 21 days before the meeting, so it is usually convenient to give notice of the meeting and of the resolution at the same time.

Notice is given when posted and assumed to be delivered, but it is safest to include a provision in the Articles that an accidental omission to give notice, or its non-receipt, will not invalidate proceedings at meetings. Usually, you do not have to give notice to shareholders living abroad.

Notice can be waived with the consent of 95 per cent of the holders of voting shares and they can agree not to meet at all, but all shareholders with voting rights must agree before you can dispense with notice of the Annual General Meeting.

Resolutions

Resolutions

Resolutions may be ordinary, special or extraordinary.

Ordinary resolutions are passed by a straight majority of those actually present at the meeting. **Special and extraordinary resolutions** need a three-quarters majority and special resolutions must include proxy votes.

Most company business, including the removal of directors and a voluntary winding up in the circumstances specified in the Articles, requires only an ordinary resolution. Special resolutions are necessary to change the Articles and the company's name or objects and reduce its capital. Extraordinary resolutions are only needed for a voluntary winding up when the company is insolvent and for reconstructions and mergers.

Copies of special and extraordinary resolutions must be sent to the Registrar within 15 days of the meeting; draft forms of resolutions are set out in Appendix 5.

De-regulation

De-regulation of private companies

Under the 1989 Companies Act it is no longer necessary to serve notice of resolutions and call and hold meetings, provided the action to be taken can be approved by the company, or any class of its shareholders, in general meeting and provided the resolution is signed by all shareholders entitled to vote at the meeting.

The provisions cover special, extraordinary and elective (see opposite) resolutions which take effect notwithstanding any provision in the Articles. The proposed written resolution must be sent to the auditors and is only valid if they endorse their statement to the effect that it does not affect them as auditors, or that it does affect them but in their opinion need not be discussed in a general or class meeting, or they make no statement within seven days of receiving it.

The resolution must be minuted as if passed in a meeting and, when signed by a director or the secretary, is evidence that it has been passed in accordance with the Act. It must be filed with the Registrar if this is required for such a resolution passed in a general or class meeting.

There are some exceptions to and adaptations of the procedure. For instance, written resolutions cannot be used to remove directors or auditors before the expiry of their term of office. Special procedural requirements apply to written resolutions for the disapplication of pre-emption rights, the provision of financial assistance to enable the company to buy its own shares, approval of payments out of capital, and of directors' service contracts and their business expenses.

Elective resolutions

Elective resolutions

This was another 1989 innovation, permitting a company to elect, with the shareholders' unanimous agreement at a properly convened general meeting, or with their written consent, to dispense with certain procedural requirements. The shareholders can jointly decide to have no Annual General Meeting, dispense with the requirement to lay accounts before shareholders and vote annually to appoint auditors. They can also give directors an indefinite authority (ie beyond the five-year limit) to allot shares and reduce the majority required for consent to short notice of meeting to 90 per cent.

◀ CHAPTER 6 ▶

CHANGES AFTER INCORPORATION

Changes made after incorporation involve formalities, and some decisions can only be made by the shareholders in general meeting and necessitate filing forms and copy documents with the Registrar.

The directors are responsible for keeping the Registrar informed and there are penalties if some of the documentation is not filed.

Some of the documentation must be signed by a director and/or the company secretary and some by the chairman of the relevant meeting. The documents you are most likely to use are discussed in this chapter and listed in Appendix 3 and draft forms of resolutions are set out in Appendix 5.

Changing directors and secretary

Change of directors and secretary

Directors are elected, re-elected and removed by a majority vote on an ordinary resolution put before the shareholders in general meeting but the shareholders do not vote on the appointment or removal of the company secretary.

Two directors can be appointed in one resolution, and notice of a resolution to prevent re-appointment or to remove or replace serving directors must be sent to shareholders at least 28 days before the meeting. Notice must also be given to the person concerned and to the auditors.

A director can put his objections to removal to the shareholders' meeting or require the company to circulate his written representations. The notice of the resolution sent to shareholders should then state that he has made written representations.

Changes of directors and secretary must be filed with the Registrar on *Form 288b* (see page 50), which incorporates a form of consent to act which must be signed by the new officer. Changes in their particulars must be filed on *Form 288c* (see page 51). It is the directors' responsibility to ensure that the Registrar is notified of a change of directors or company secretary.

Changing the auditors

Changing auditors

An auditor is appointed at each Annual General Meeting to hold office from the conclusion of the meeting until the conclusion of the next Annual General Meeting. He must be a member of the Institute of Chartered Accountants in England and Wales, Scotland or Ireland or a member of the Association of Certified and Corporate Accountants (see page 78). Remuneration, including expenses, is fixed by the shareholders in general meeting.

Appointment is by ordinary resolution of the shareholders and can be made at any time before the expiry of the term of office agreed separately with the directors, so that the auditor may be entitled to compensation for premature termination of the separate agreement.

A retiring auditor or one removed before the expiration of his term of office may address the meeting called to appoint his successor, or require the company to circulate his comments to shareholders, and the resolution for his replacement should state that he has made written representations. He is also entitled to attend company meetings which discuss matters dealt with during his term of office.

The directors or the company in general meeting can fill casual vacancies but the appointment must be confirmed by resolution at the Annual General Meeting. Unless the court orders otherwise, a copy of the auditor's statement must be sent to the Registrar.

Special notice of 28 days is required for resolutions appointing new

COMPANIES HOUSE

Please complete in typescript, or in bold black capitals.

391

Notice of passing of resolution removing an auditor

Company Number

Company Name in full

```
*F391001T*
```

	Day	Month	Year
Date of resolution			

	Day	Month	Year
Date of removal			

Details of auditor removed from office

Firm / Partnership / Individual

Address

Post town

County / Region   Postcode

Signed   **Date**

† Please delete as appropriate.

† a director / secretary

Please give the name, address, telephone number and, if available, a DX number and Exchange of the person Companies House should contact if there is any query.

Tel

DX number   DX exchange

Companies House receipt date barcode

When you have completed and signed the form please send it to the Registrar of Companies at:

Companies House, Crown Way, Cardiff, CF4 3UZ   DX 33050 Cardiff
for companies registered in England and Wales
or
Companies House, 37 Castle Terrace, Edinburgh, EH1 2EB
for companies registered in Scotland   **DX 235 Edinburgh**

Form revised March 1995

COMPANIES HOUSE

Please complete in typescript,
or in bold black capitals.

287

Change in situation or address of Registered Office

Company Number

Company Name in full

F287001X

New situation of registered office

NOTE:

The change in the
situation of the
registered office does
not take effect until the
Registrar has registered
this notice.

For 14 days beginning
with the date that a
change of registered
office is registered, a
person may validly serve
any document on the
company at its previous
registered office.

PO Box numbers only
are not acceptable.

Address

Post town

County / Region

Postcode

Signed

Date

† Please delete as appropriate.

Please give the name, address,
telephone number and, if available,
a DX number and Exchange of
the person Companies House should
contact if there is any query.

† a director / secretary / administrator / administrative receiver / liquidator / receiver manager / receiver

Tel

DX number   DX exchange

Companies House receipt date barcode

Form revised March 1995

When you have completed and signed the form please send it to the
Registrar of Companies at:
Companies House, Crown Way, Cardiff, CF4 3UZ   DX 33050 Cardiff
for companies registered in England and Wales
or
Companies House, 37 Castle Terrace, Edinburgh, EH1 2EB
for companies registered in Scotland   **DX 235 Edinburgh**

89

auditors, and to reappoint an auditor appointed to fill a casual vacancy or to remove one before expiry of his term of office.

Notice of removal of the auditors must be sent to the Registrar on *Form 391* (see page 88) within 14 days of the meeting.

The auditor is entitled to attend all meetings of the company and to receive all notes of, and other communications relating to, meetings which are sent to shareholders.

Changing the registered office

Change of registered office

Changes must be notified to the Registrar, within 14 days of the change, on *Form 287* (see page 89).

Change in the place where statutory books and other 'public' documents are kept

Notices of any change in the place where the Register of Members (*Form 353* – see page 91), copies of directors' service contracts (*Form 318* – see page 92) and their interests in shares (*Form 325* – see page 93) are kept must be filed with the Registrar within 14 days of the change. No time limit is specified for filing a notice of a change in the place where the Register of Debenture Holders (*Form 190* – see page 94) is kept.

Changing the company's name

Change of name

The company's name is changed by majority vote of the shareholders on a special resolution. A copy of the signed resolution must be sent to the Registrar within 15 days of the meeting with the £20 fee for entry on the Index or £200 for a same-day change. The restrictions on your choice are set out in Appendix 1 and the change is effective from the date of the issue by the Registrar of an altered Certificate of Incorporation.

Changes to the capital of the company

Increases in capital and allotment of shares

The company's authorised capital can be increased by ordinary resolution authorising the increase. A copy of the signed resolution and *Form 123* (see page 95) must be sent to the Registrar within 15 days of the resolution and no capital duty is payable.

COMPANIES HOUSE

Please complete in typescript,
or in bold black capitals.

Register of members

353

When the
register of
members is kept
in a non-legible
form, Companies
Form 353a (not
illustrated) gives
notice of the
place where it
may be
inspected.

Company Number

Company Name in full

F 3 5 3 0 0 1 R

The register of members is kept at:

NOTE:
The register **MUST** be kept at an address in the country of incorporation.

This notice is not required where the register has, at all times since it came into existence (or in the case of a register in existence on 1 July 1948 at all times since then) been kept at the registered office.

Address

Post town

County / Region   Postcode

Signed   **Date**

† Please delete as appropriate.

Please give the name, address, telephone number and, if available, a DX number and Exchange of the person Companies House should contact if there is any query.

† a director / secretary / administrator / administrative receiver / receiver manager / receiver

Tel

DX number   DX exchange

Companies House receipt date barcode

When you have completed and signed the form please send it to the Registrar of Companies at:
Companies House, Crown Way, Cardiff, CF4 3UZ   DX 33050 Cardiff
for companies registered in England and Wales
or
Companies House, 37 Castle Terrace, Edinburgh, EH1 2EB
for companies registered in Scotland   **DX 235 Edinburgh**

Form revised March 1995

91

COMPANIES HOUSE

*Please complete in typescript,
or in bold black capitals.*

318

Location of directors' service contracts

Company Number

Company Name in full

✳F3180015✳

Address where directors' service contracts
or memoranda are available for inspection
by members.

NOTE:
Directors' service
contracts **MUST** be kept
at an address in the
country of incorporation.

This notice is not
required where the
relevant documents are
and have always been
kept at the Registered
Office.

Address

Post town

County / Region   Postcode

Signed   **Date**

† Please delete as appropriate.

† a director / secretary / administrator / administrative receiver / receiver manager / receiver

Please give the name, address,
telephone number and, if available,
a DX number and Exchange of
the person Companies House should
contact if there is any query.

Tel

DX number   DX exchange

When you have completed and signed the form please send it to the
Registrar of Companies at:
Companies House, Crown Way, Cardiff, CF4 3UZ   DX 33050 Cardiff
for companies registered in England and Wales
or
Companies House, 37 Castle Terrace, Edinburgh, EH1 2EB
for companies registered in Scotland   **DX 235 Edinburgh**

Form revised March 1995

COMPANIES HOUSE

Please complete in typescript, or in bold black capitals.

325

Location of register of directors' interests in shares etc.

Company Number

Company Name in full

✱F 3 2 5 0 0 1 0 ✱

When the register of directors' interests is kept in a non-legible form, Companies Form 325a (not illustrated) gives notice of the place where it may be inspected.

The register of directors' interests in shares and/or debentures is kept at:

NOTE:
The register **MUST** be kept at an address in the country of incorporation.

This notice is not required where the register is and has always been kept at the Registered Office.

Address

Post town

County / Region   Postcode

Signed   Date

† Please delete as appropriate.

Please give the name, address, telephone number and, if available, a DX number and Exchange of the person Companies House should contact if there is any query.

† a director / secretary / administrator / administrative receiver / receiver manager / receiver

Tel

DX number   DX exchange

When you have completed and signed the form please send it to the Registrar of Companies at:
Companies House, Crown Way, Cardiff, CF4 3UZ   DX 33050 Cardiff
for companies registered in England and Wales
or
Companies House, 37 Castle Terrace, Edinburgh, EH1 2EB
for companies registered in Scotland   **DX 235 Edinburgh**

Form revised March 1995

When the register of debenture holders is kept in a non-legible form, Companies Form 190a (not illustrated) gives notice of the place where it may be inspected.

COMPANIES HOUSE

Please complete in typescript, or in bold black capitals.

190

Location of register of debenture holders

Company Number

Company Name in full

F 1 9 0 0 0 1 0

NOTE:
This notice is not required where the register is, and has always been, kept at the Registered Office

gives notice that †[a register][registers]†[in duplicate form] of holders of debentures of the company of the classes mentioned below †[is][are]kept at:

Address

Post town

County / region

Postcode

Brief description of class of debentures

Signed

Date

† Please delete as appropriate.

† a director / secretary

Please give the name, address, telephone number and, if available, a DX number and Exchange of the person Companies House should contact if there is any query.

Tel

DX number   DX exchange

When you have completed and signed the form please send it to the Registrar of Companies at:
Companies House, Crown Way, Cardiff, CF4 3UZ   DX 33050 Cardiff
for companies registered in England and Wales
or
Companies House, 37 Castle Terrace, Edinburgh, EH1 2EB
for companies registered in Scotland   **DX 235 Edinburgh**

Form revised March 1995

G

COMPANIES FORM No. 123

Notice of increase in nominal capital

123

Please do not write in this margin

Pursuant to section 123 of the Companies Act 1985

Please complete legibly, preferably in black type, or bold block lettering

To the Registrar of Companies **(Address overleaf)**

For official use

Company number

* insert full name of company

Name of company

*

gives notice in accordance with section 123 of the above Act that by resolution of the company

dated _____the nominal capital of the company has been

§ the copy must be printed or in some other form approved by the registrar

increased by £ _____ beyond the registered capital of £ _____.

A copy of the resolution authorising the increase is attached.§

The conditions (eg. voting rights, dividend rights, winding-up rights etc.) subject to which the new

shares have been or are to be issued are as follow:

Please tick here if continued overleaf

‡ Insert Director, Secretary, Administrator, Administrative Receiver or Receiver (Scotland) as appropriate

Signed

Designation‡

Date

Presentor's name address and reference (if any):

For official Use

General Section

Post room

G

COMPANIES FORM No. 88(2)(Rev 1988)

Return of allotments of shares

Pursuant to section 88(2) of the Companies Act 1985 (the Act)

88(2)

(REVISED 1988)

This form replaces forms PUC2, PUC3 and 88(2)

Please do not write in this margin

To the Registrar of Companies (**address overleaf**) (see note 1)

Please complete legibly, preferably in black type, or bold block lettering

Company number

* insert full name of company

1. Name of company

*

2. This section must be completed for all allotments

† distinguish between ordinary preference, etc.

Description of shares †			
A Number allotted			
B Nominal value of each	£	£	£
C Total amount (if any) paid or due and payable on each share (including premium if any)	£	£	£

§ complete (a) or (b) as appropriate

Date(s) on which the shares were allotted

(a) [on _____ 19 _____] §, or

(b) [from _____ 19 _____ to _____ 19 _____ .] §

The names and addresses of the allottees and the number of shares allotted to each should be given overleaf

3. If the allotment is wholly or partly other than for cash the following information must be given (**see notes 2 & 3**)

D Extent to which each share is to be treated as paid up. Please use percentage.			

E Consideration for which the shares were allotted _____

_____

_____

NOTES

1. This form should be delivered to the Registrar of Companies within one month of the (first) date of allotment.

2. If the allotment is wholly or partly other than for cash, the company must deliver to the registrar a return containing the information at D & E. The company may deliver this information by completing D & E and the delivery of the information must be accompanied by the duly stamped contract required by section 88(2)(b) of the Act or by the duly stamped prescribed particulars required by section 88(3) (Form No 88(3)).

3. Details of bonus issues should be included only in section 2.

Presentor's name address, telephone number and reference (if any):

For official use

Post room

Page 1

Within a month of the allotment of shares a Return of Allotments form, signed by a director or the secretary, must be filed with the Registrar. If the shares are issued for cash, the form to be completed is *88(2)* – see page 96; otherwise *Form 88(3)* – see page 34 – must be filed together with a copy of the contract of sale or details specified on the form. Duty is then payable at the rate of £1 per £100 or part of £100 but no duty is payable if the company makes a bonus issue of shares out of undistributed profits.

If the new issue varies the rights of existing shareholders it should be done through a **scheme of arrangement**, whether their rights are contained in the Memorandum or the Articles. The procedure involves an application to the court so you should take expert advice before taking action; dissenting shareholders can put their objections to the variation both to the court and to the shareholders' meeting.

The directors' authority to allot shares

The directors' authority to allot shares expires five years from the date of incorporation or not more than five years after the date of adoption of an Article giving them the authority. Giving them authority, or varying, revoking or renewing it, requires the written consent of three-quarters of the shareholders or their consent given on an extraordinary resolution in general meeting.

The resolution must state or restate the amount of shares which may be allotted under the authority, or the amount remaining to be allotted under it, and must specify the date on which an authority or amended authority will expire. A copy of the signed resolution must be sent to the Registrar within 15 days of the passing of the resolution.

Changes in the Memorandum of Association

Changing the Memorandum and Articles of Association

Alteration of the **objects clause** requires the approval of 75 per cent of the shareholders to a special resolution.

Application to cancel the alteration can be made to the court within 21 days of the resolution by the holders of 15 per cent of the shares. If there is no objection the alteration is valid and a printed copy of the amended Memorandum, together with a copy of the signed resolution authorising the change, must be sent to the Registrar, but the change is not effective until the Registrar has advertised it in the *Gazette*.

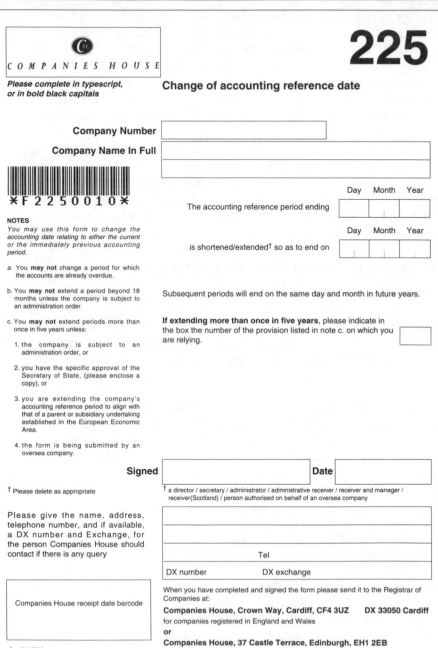

COMPANIES HOUSE

*Please complete in typescript,
or in bold black capitals*

225

Change of accounting reference date

Company Number

Company Name In Full

F2250010

NOTES

*You may use this form to change the
accounting date relating to either the current
or the immediately previous accounting
period.*

a. You **may not** change a period for which
the accounts are already overdue.

b. You **may not** extend a period beyond 18
months unless the company is subject to
an administration order.

c. You **may not** extend periods more than
once in five years unless:

1. the company is subject to an
administration order, or

2. you have the specific approval of the
Secretary of State, (please enclose a
copy), or

3. you are extending the company's
accounting reference period to align with
that of a parent or subsidiary undertaking
established in the European Economic
Area.

4. the form is being submitted by an
oversea company.

	Day	Month	Year
The accounting reference period ending			

	Day	Month	Year
is shortened/extended† so as to end on			

Subsequent periods will end on the same day and month in future years.

If extending more than once in five years, please indicate in
the box the number of the provision listed in note c. on which you
are relying.

Signed   **Date**

† Please delete as appropriate

† a director / secretary / administrator / administrative receiver / receiver and manager /
receiver(Scotland) / person authorised on behalf of an oversea company

Please give the name, address,
telephone number, and if available,
a DX number and Exchange, for
the person Companies House should
contact if there is any query

Tel

DX number   DX exchange

Companies House receipt date barcode

When you have completed and signed the form please send it to the Registrar of
Companies at:

Companies House, Crown Way, Cardiff, CF4 3UZ   DX 33050 Cardiff
for companies registered in England and Wales
or
Companies House, 37 Castle Terrace, Edinburgh, EH1 2EB
for companies registered in Scotland   **DX 235 Edinburgh**

April 1996

Changes in the Articles of Association

Alterations in the Articles are by a majority vote of the shareholders on a special resolution but if the company has two or more classes of shares, and the alteration affects the rights attached to any class, it should be done through a scheme of arrangement.

Printed and signed copies of resolutions altering the Articles must be sent to the Registrar within 15 days of the resolution but the alteration is not effective until the Registrar has advertised it in the *Gazette*.

Changing the accounting reference date

You can change the ARD by shortening or extending (to a maximum of 18 months) the accounting period (which fixes your accounting year). The change must be made during a current period and details must be sent to the Registrar on *Form 225(1)* – see page 98. No time limit is specified but it must be sent before the end of the period.

The **annual return** is sent to the Registrar on *Form 363a* (see page 68), signed by a director *or* the secretary. It must be made up to the 'return date', which is the anniversary of incorporation or, if the last return was made up to a different date, on the anniversary of that date.

Striking the company off the Register

Failure to file returns or accounts may lead to an enquiry as to whether the company has ceased trading and the Registrar may delete the company from the Register if:

- up-to date information about the company's activities has not been filed, or
- there are no effective officers, or
- mail sent to the registered office is returned undelivered, or
- information is received that the company has ceased trading.

Before taking action the Registrar writes to the company to make enquiries. Failing a response, he then informs the company, and publishes notice in the *Gazette*, of his intention to strike the company off after three months unless cause is shown to the contrary. Before striking off, the Registrar considers the objections of creditors and may delay taking action in order to allow them to pursue their claims and to petition to wind up the company. Notice of striking off will then be published in the *Gazette*. If there are assets they are *bona vacantia*, that is, they belong to either the Crown or the Duchy of Lancaster or the Duchy of Cornwall, depending on the location of the registered office.

◀ CHAPTER 7 ▶

INSOLVENCY

Limited liability means that if the business is insolvent, management's only liability is for fraud and for recklessness and incompetence which has jeopardised the interests of the creditors.

This chapter summarises the various procedures for winding up the company, but if drastic decisions must be made you should take expert advice. All the procedures require reference to, and action by, an insolvency practitioner, who must be a member of a recognised professional body such as the Institute of Chartered Accountants or the Law Society, or authorised by the Secretary of State. They involve formalities, meetings of shareholders and creditors, time limits, reporting to and filing documentation with the Registrar, and publicity; there are fines and penalties if you do not comply with the statutory requirements.

When a company is insolvent

Legal insolvency

A company is legally insolvent if it is unable to pay its debts and discharge its liabilities as and when they fall due, or the value of its assets is less than its liabilities. In determining liabilities, contingent and prospective liabilities must be taken into account, as well as actual and quantified amounts. Day-to-day involvement in management often gives a false picture of the company's financial position and if customers are slow to pay, plant, machinery and stock have been purchased under credit agreements and the company's bank account is in overdraft, the business may be far from healthy, however heavy the order book.

Financial problems need not, however, lead to liquidation. The procedures introduced by the 1986 Insolvency Act permit a company to reach a compromise agreement with creditors, or to apply to the court for an administration order, so that company affairs can be reorganised and supervised and insolvency avoided.

You should therefore ensure that you have adequate accounting records and proper financial advice so that you are able to consider taking appropriate action.

Voluntary striking off

If a company has effectively ceased to operate, the Registrar may consider a written request to strike the company off the Register. If the company is struck off any remaining assets pass to the Crown, the Duchy of Lancaster or the Duchy of Cornwall, depending on the location of the registered office. If there are debts, the creditors can object and, in any event, the directors', management's and shareholders' liability continues as if the company had not been dissolved.

Arrangements with creditors

Voluntary arrangements: compositions and schemes of arrangement

These procedures offer a relatively straightforward method whereby a potentially solvent company concludes a legally effective arrangement with creditors with minimum reference to the court.

Procedure

The directors or the liquidator or administrator (see below) put a statement of affairs – which sets out the company's financial position – and detailed proposals to creditors and shareholders for a **scheme** or **composition** in satisfaction of debts. They must nominate an insolvency practitioner to supervise the arrangement and, unless he is a liquidator or administrator, he must report to the court as to the necessity for shareholders' and creditors' meetings and notify creditors. A liquidator or administrator must call meetings but need not report to court. The meetings must approve the supervisor and can accept, modify or reject the proposals. Secured and preferred creditors are protected; directors, shareholders, creditors and the supervisor can challenge decisions and implementation.

The arrangement is carried out by the supervisor and he can refer to the court, which can stay (stop) the winding up and discharge an administration order.

Administration orders

This procedure is mainly for companies which do not borrow on standard fixed and floating charges and enables a potentially or actually insolvent company to put its affairs in the hands of an administrator, so that part or all of the company can be salvaged or a more advantageous realisation of assets can be secured than on a winding up.

Application is made to the court, which must be satisfied that the company is, or is likely to become, unable to pay its debts. In addition, the court must consider that the order would be likely to enable part or all of the undertaking to survive as a going concern, and/or creditors are likely to agree a satisfactory arrangement with the company, and/or realisation of the assets is likely to be more advantageous than if the company were wound up.

The order can be used together with a voluntary arrangement or compromise or arrangement with creditors under the Companies Acts but not if the company is already in liquidation.

The petition is presented to the court by the company and/or directors and/or creditors and notice must be given to debenture holders who have appointed, or have the right to appoint, an administrative receiver under a floating charge. On presentation of the petition, the administrator takes over management and no legal proceedings can issue or continue against the company, but an administrative receiver can be appointed and a petition for winding up can be presented. A more detailed statement of affairs verified on affidavit by current and former officers of the company and, in some circumstances, employees, is drawn up and the administrator's proposals for reorganisation, which depend on the terms of the court order, can be rejected by shareholders, creditors or the court although the creditors' approval is not mandatory.

Receivership

This is the procedure by which assets secured by a floating charge are realised. Secured creditors can enforce their security independently of a winding up and without regard to the unsecured creditors or to the interests of the company.

Administrative receivers are appointed under a debenture secured by a charge and the appointment can be over all or a substantial part of the company's assets. The appointment can be by the debenture holders or the court, and again the administrative receiver takes over management.

Receivers are appointed under the terms of a fixed charge or by the court but they cannot act as administrative receivers. Their powers depend on the terms of the charge or court order and the appointment suspends the fixed charge holders' right to enforce their security without the consent of the court or administrator, who can dispose of the charged property, giving them the same priority as they would have had if they had enforced the charge directly.

Receivers and directors

The directors' powers effectively cease when a receiver or administrative receiver is appointed. A receiver ceases to act when he has sufficient funds to discharge the debt due to his appointor and his expenses but an administrative receiver can only be removed by court order.

Bringing the company's operations to an end

Winding up

This is the statutory procedure which brings a company's operations to an end, realising the assets and distributing the proceeds among creditors and shareholders in accordance with their rights. The company is then dissolved.

A company can be wound up compulsorily by court order or voluntarily by the shareholders if it is insolvent, or by shareholders if it is solvent.

Voluntary winding up

The company puts itself into voluntary liquidation by passing a resolution at a general meeting of the shareholders. Seven days' notice of the meeting must be given and a notice of a creditors' meeting to be held on the same day or the day after must be sent on the same date.

The decision can be by ordinary resolution if the company was formed for a fixed period or a specific undertaking; otherwise a special resolution must be passed. An extraordinary resolution is necessary if the company is insolvent.

Voluntary liquidation

A members' or shareholders' voluntary liquidation requires the majority of the directors to prepare a declaration of solvency after full enquiry into the company's affairs. The declaration sets out the company's assets and liabilities and states that it will be able to pay its debts within, at most, 12 months; if they are not paid, the directors may be liable to a fine or imprisonment.

If no declaration is made or the liquidator disagrees with its conclusion or the company cannot pay its debts within 12 months, it becomes a creditors' voluntary liquidation and the creditors appoint and can supervise the liquidator.

The advantage of a voluntary liquidation is that although employees are dismissed if the company is insolvent, the directors can continue to act provided they have the approval of the liquidator and of the shareholders given in general meeting; in a creditors' voluntary liquidation the creditors must also give their consent.

If the resolution is passed without appointing a liquidator, the directors can dispose of perishable goods and those likely to diminish in value unless immediately disposed of, and take action necessary to protect company assets until one is appointed. Any further action requires the consent of the court, and the company must stop trading except in so far as may be required for beneficial winding up.

The liquidation starts on the date the resolution for winding up is passed; if the liquidator thinks the company is insolvent, the winding up continues as a creditors' voluntary liquidation. The liquidator stays in office until removed after his final report to shareholders and creditors but he can resign or vacate office on notice to the Registrar of the final meeting.

Distribution of
assets

Distribution

Available assets are applied against the company's liabilities, and shareholders are only called on for any balance remaining unpaid on their shares.

Creditors' rights

Fixed chargeholders take the first slice of the assets, followed by liquidation expenses, preferential debts, floating chargeholders and sums due to shareholders (for instance arrears of dividend), although in some circumstances floating chargeholders may have prior claims to holders of a fixed charge (see page 41). Remaining assets go to unsecured creditors, who can claim interest to the date of distribution, and any surplus is divided among shareholders in accordance with their rights under the Memorandum and Articles of Association.

Preferential debts comprise outstanding tax to a maximum of 12 months, including PAYE; contributions in respect of subcontractors in the construction industry; six months' VAT; general betting duty; 12 months' National Insurance contributions; state and occupational pension scheme contributions; arrears of wages for four months (including directors but not the managing director) to a maximum of £205 per week, including Statutory Sick Pay, protective awards, payment during medical suspension, time off work and accrued holiday pay. Wages Act employee claims are paid if the company has more than ten employees and most amounts payable to employees under the employment legislation can be reimbursed partly or wholly from the Redundancy Fund. Employees can claim for any balance still outstanding with the ordinary (unsecured) creditors.

Dissolution in a voluntary liquidation

The company is dissolved three months from registration by the Registrar of the liquidator's final account and return.

Compulsory winding up

The compulsory procedure can be initiated by the company, a

shareholder, a creditor, the official receiver (employed by the Department of Trade and Industry), or the Department of Trade and Industry.

The most frequent basis for the petition is insolvency, which here is presumed if a creditor has been owed at least £750 for more than three weeks after a formal demand has been served, or the company has not discharged a judgment debt or court order. The court appoints a liquidator who can, without reference to the court or creditors, take over management of the company forthwith. Here the liquidator not only gets in and distributes the assets but also must provide the official receiver with any information and documents he requires. The official receiver must look into the cause of the company's failure, reporting if necessary to the court, and he can apply for public examination of officers, liquidators, administrators and anyone else involved in the company's affairs.

Fines and penalties

If the company has been trading with an intent to defraud creditors or anyone else, or incurring debts without a reasonable prospect of repayment, anyone involved may be prosecuted and disqualified from participating directly or indirectly in the management of a company for a maximum of 15 years. Conviction for an indictable offence (that is, a serious offence triable by jury in the Crown Court) relating to the promotion, formation, management or liquidation of a company, or with the receivership or management of its property, or for persistent failure to file accounts and records, can also lead to disqualification.

Fraudulent and wrongful trading can in addition bring a personal liability for all the company's debts. Fraudulent trading is trading with an intent to defraud creditors and, if the company is in insolvent liquidation and a director, *de facto*, or shadow director knew, or should have known, that there was no reasonable prospect that the company could have avoided insolvent liquidation, there may also be criminal liability for wrongful trading and disqualification.

Officers of the company and anyone else acting in the promotion, formation, management or liquidation of a company in liquidation are personally liable if they retain or misapply assets or they are in breach of duty to the company.

Voidable transactions: preferences and transactions at an undervalue

Any transaction entered into by an insolvent company which puts a creditor, surety or guarantor into a better position than he would be in the liquidation may be voidable and set aside as a 'preference'. The preference may be a transaction at a proper price or at an undervalue (that is, a gratuitous gift or transfer or one made for significantly less than market value). The risk period dates back from presentation of a petition for an administrative order or the date the order is made, or the commencement of liquidation.

Transactions at a proper price or an undervalue are safe if made in good faith and for the purpose of carrying on the business, provided that at the time there were reasonable grounds that the transaction would benefit the company. They are at risk, however, if made at a time when the company was unable to pay its debts or it became unable to pay them as a result of the transaction. Preferences at an undervalue and any preference, even one at a proper price, with a connected person is at risk for two years; there is a six-month risk period for other preferences and preferences made in the period prior to the making of an administration order.

The network of connected persons here extends to cover directors, shadow directors (persons in accordance with whose instructions directors are accustomed to act), company officers and their spouses, including a former and reputed spouse, and their children and step-children, as well as their partners, a company with which they are associated and of which they control at least one-fifth of the voting shares and a trustee of any trust under which they, their family group, or associated company is a beneficiary.

Floating charges may also be voidable. They are valid whenever created to the extent that consideration (that is, payment in cash, goods or services or in discharge of debts) is received by the company. The balance is at risk for one year if made when the company was unable to pay its debts, and two years if made in favour of a connected person.

Distribution is on the same basis as in voluntary liquidation.

Dissolution in compulsory winding up

The liquidator reports to a final meeting of creditors when winding up is completed; if the official receiver is acting, he can apply for early dissolution on the basis that assets will not cover winding up expenses and no further investigation is required. Three months from the date of registration of dissolution entered by the Registrar, the company is dissolved.

Restriction on use of the company name

Directors and shadow directors acting within 12 months of insolvent liquidation cannot act for, or be involved with, a company with the same name. Nor can they for five years use a former name or trading name used during the previous 12 months or one so similar as to suggest continuing association, without the consent of the court. Non-compliance brings a personal joint and several liability with the company and anyone acting on the offender's instructions.

◀ CHAPTER 8 ▶

THE READY-MADE COMPANY

Buying a company off the shelf

The fastest way to incorporation is to buy an 'off the shelf', ready-made company already registered at Companies House from your solicitor or accountant or one of the many registration agents who advertise in financial and professional journals. All the necessary documentation will have been filed with the Registrar and the company will have a Certificate of Incorporation, so that it can start trading as soon as you have appointed your own director(s) and secretary and transferred the shares to your own shareholders.

Companies House offer an incorporation service for £50; agents' fees are about £150 inclusive of VAT. If you use agents, you are advised to use members of the Association of Company Registration Agents, and if you want to choose your own company name they will check its availability for a fee. If you intend to use the name as a trade mark, you should also carry out a search at the Trade Marks Registry in the appropriate class of goods and services.

Companies House will send you information packs and guides and agents will advise you on the necessary initial changes for takeover. The objects clause can be changed but you should ensure that the existing principal objects clause covers your main business activities.

You will then have a company with a current Certificate of Incorporation, a standard Memorandum of Association with an appropriate objects and capital clause, standard Articles of Association, a set of statutory books and a company seal if this is required by your Articles, for a cost of about £150 including VAT. The existing directors, secretary and shareholders of the ready-made company, usually the agent's nominees, resign in favour of your nominees.

If the nominee shareholders were companies, your ready-made company cannot claim exemption from audit for its accounts (see page 75), unless it is dormant throughout its first financial year. It may therefore be worthwhile shortening the first accounting period so it ends on the day on which you take ownership of the shares (see page 99). The company must, however, pass a special resolution not to appoint auditors and deliver dormant company accounts for the first (shortened) period, before the first general meeting at which accounts are laid.

You may wish to make other changes, which must be notified to the Registrar of Companies in accordance with the Companies Act and which are dealt with in Chapter 6. These involve some delay but the procedure is more straightforward and less expensive than starting from scratch.

◀ APPENDIX 1 ▶

NOTES FOR GUIDANCE ON COMPANY NAMES

A. Use of the following words and expressions in a company or business name requires the prior approval of the Secretary of State for Trade and Industry:

(a) *Words which imply national or international pre-eminence*

International	British	Wales
National	England	Welsh
European	English	Ireland
United Kingdom	Scotland	Irish
Great Britain	Scottish	

(b) *Words which imply governmental patronage or sponsorship*

Authority	Board	Council

(c) *Words which imply business pre-eminence or representative status*

Association	Society	Institute
Federation		Institution

(d) *Words which imply specific objects or functions*

Assurance	Chamber of Commerce	Group
Insurance	Chamber of Commerce,	Holding
Reinsurance	Training and Enterprise	Building Society
Reassurance	Chemist	Trade Union
Insurer	Chemistry	Foundation

Fund	Chamber of Industry	Charter
Charity	Post Office	Chartered
Assurer	Giro	Co-operative
Reassurer	Register	Stock Exchange
Reinsurer	Registered	Trust
Patent	Friendly Society	Benevolent
Patentee	Industrial & Provident	Sheffield
Chamber of Trade	Society	

B. Use of the following words and expressions also requires the prior consent of the relevant body as well as the Secretary of State. A statement that a written request has been made to the relevant body seeking its opinion as to use of the word or expression must be filed with the application for registration, together with a copy of any response:

Word or expression	Relevant body for persons intending to set up business in England or Wales	Relevant body for persons intending to set up business in Scotland
Royal, Royale, Royalty, King, Queen, Prince, Princess, Windsor, Duke, His/Her Majesty	'A' Division (Room 730), Home Office, Queen Anne's Gate, London SW1H 9AT (if based in England) Welsh Office, Cathay Park, Cardiff CF1 3NQ (if based in Wales)	Scottish Home and Health Department, Old St Andrews House, Edinburgh EH1 3DE
Police	Home Office, F1 Division, Police Department, Queen Anne's Gate, London SW1H 9AT	As above
Special School	Department for Education and Employment, Schools 1C Branch, Sanctuary Buildings, Great Smith Street, London SW1P 3BT	As for England and Wales

Word or expression	Relevant body for persons intending to set up business in England or Wales	Relevant body for persons intending to set up business in Scotland
Contact Lens	General Optical Council, 41 Harley Street, London W1N 2DJ	As for England and Wales
Dental, Dentistry	General Dental Council, 37 Wimpole Street, London W1M 8DQ	As for England and Wales
District Nurse, Health Visitor, Midwife, Midwifery Nurse, Nursing	United Kingdom Central Council for Nursing, Midwifery and Health Visiting, 23 Portland Place, London W1N 3AF	As for England and Wales
Health Centre	Department of Health, PMC 1C Division, Alexander Fleming House, Elephant and Castle, London SE1 6TE	As for England and Wales
Health Service	Department of Health, H52B Division, Eileen House, 80–94 Newington Causeway, London SE1 6EF	As for England and Wales
Pregnancy, Termination, Abortion	Department of Health, PMC 2A Division, Room B1204, Alexander Fleming House, Elephant and Castle, London SE1 6TE	As for England and Wales

Word or expression	Relevant body for persons intending to set up business in England or Wales	Relevant body for persons intending to set up business in Scotland
Charity, Charitable	Charity Commission, Registration Division, 14 Ryder Street, St James's, London SW1Y 6AH	Scottish Home and Health Department, Civil Law and Charities Division, St Andrews House, Edinburgh EH1 3DE
Apothecary	The Worshipful Society of Apothecaries of London, Apothecaries Hall, Blackfriars Lane, London EC4V 6EJ	The Pharmaceutical Society of Great Britain, Law Department, 1 Lambeth High Street, London SE1 7JN
University, Polytechnic	Department for Education and Employment, FH3 Division, Sanctuary Buildings, Great Smith Street, London SW1P 3BT	As for England and Wales

C. The use of certain words is covered by other legislation and may constitute a criminal offence. Some of these words are listed below but the list is not exhaustive. If you wish to use any of them, you should seek legal advice and confirmation from the body concerned that the use of the word does not contravene the relevant legislation, but their opinion is not conclusive:

Word or expression	Appropriate body
Architect, Architectural	Architects Registration Council of the United Kingdom, 73 Hallam Street, London W1N 6EE
Credit Union	The Registry of Friendly Societies, 15–17 Great Marlborough Street, London W1V 2AX
Dentist, Dental Surgeon, Dental Practitioner	General Dental Council, 37 Wimpole Street, London W1M 8DQ

Word or expression	Appropriate body
Veterinary Surgeon, Veterinary, Vet	Royal College of Veterinary Surgeons, Belgravia House, 62–64 Horseferry Road, London SW1P 2AF
Drug, Druggist, Pharmaceutical, Pharmaceutist, Pharmacist, Pharmacy	The Pharmaceutical Society of Great Britain, Law Department, 1 Lambeth High Street, London SE1 7JN
Optician, Ophthalmic Optician, Dispensing Optician, Enrolled Optician, Registered Optician, Optometrist	General Optical Council, 41 Harley Street, London W1N 2DJ
Bank, Banker, Banking Deposit	Bank of England, Threadneedle Street, London EC2R 8AH
Red Cross	Seek advice of Companies House
Anzac	Seek advice of Companies House
Insurance Broker, Assurance Broker, Re-Insurance Broker, Reassurance Broker	Insurance Brokers Registration Council, 15 St Helen's Place, London EC3A 6DS
* Chiropodist, * Dietician, * Medical Laboratory Technician * Occupational Therapist, * Orthoptist, * Physiotherapist, * Radiographer, * Remedial Gymnast	Room 1226, HAP4 Division, Department of Health, Hannibal House, Elephant and Castle, London SE1 6TE

* Where preceded by the words Registered, State Registered, State.

Institute of Laryngology, Institute of Otology, Institute of Utology, Institute of Orthopaedics	Seek advice of University College, London

Word or expression	Appropriate body
Patent Office, Patent Agent	IPCD, Hazlitt House, 45 Southampton Buildings, London WC2A 1AY and IPCD, Government Buildings, Cardiff Road, Newport, Gwent
Building Society	Seek advice of Building Society Commission, 15–17 Great Marlborough Street, London W1V 2AX

Only persons carrying on business as a building society in the UK may use a name which implies that they are in any way connected with the business of a building society.

D. 'Too like' names – The Secretary of State takes account of facts which might suggest similarity and lead to confusion including, for instance, the nature and location of a business. Evidence to show confusion is taken into account.

E. A name suggesting a connection with a company already on the Index – The Secretary of State does not consider 'implied association' – ie whether the company might be thought to be a member of, or associated with, another company or group. Nor is consideration given to trading names, logos, trade or service marks, copyrights, patents, etc or any other proprietary rights existing in names or parts of names.

F. Company letterhead – Business owned by a company:

Bert's Shoes
6 Tuppeny Passage, London NW12 5TT

† Bert's Shoes (UK) Limited
Registered in England and Wales
Registration Number: 123456789
Registered Office: 81 Florin Way, London NW13 7DD

† Information required to be disclosed by the Business Names Act 1985 and the Companies Act 1985.

◀ APPENDIX 2 ▶

DOCUMENTS TO BE FILED ON INCORPORATION BY A PRIVATE LIMITED LIABILITY COMPANY

1. MEMORANDUM OF ASSOCIATION, stating the company's name, the situation of its registered office (England, Scotland or Wales), the objects for which the company is formed and the powers taken by the company, that the liability of the shareholders is limited and the amount of the share capital divided into shares of a fixed amount.

   It must be dated and subscribed by not less than two persons (the subscribers), their signatures duly witnessed.

2. ARTICLES OF ASSOCIATION (unless Table A is adopted), setting out the regulations governing the company's internal affairs. This must be printed, dated and signed by the subscribers to the Memorandum and their signatures duly witnessed.

3. Statement of First Directors and Secretary and Intended Situation of Registered Office (Form 10). The form can be signed by the subscribers to the Memorandum or by agents acting on their behalf and sets out the prescribed details of the directors and secretary, who must also sign the form confirming their consent to act.

4. Declaration of Compliance with the Requirements on Application for Registration of a Company (Form 12). This can be made by a director or secretary named in the Statement of first officers above or by a solicitor engaged in the company's formation.

◄ APPENDIX 3 ►

DOCUMENTS WHICH MUST BE LODGED WITH THE REGISTRAR*

Document	Form	Signatories	When lodged	Penalty
Statement of first directors, secretary, and intended situation of registered office	10	Subscribers or their agent and each officer	Before registration	None
Declaration of compliance with requirements on application for registration	12	Director, secretary or solicitor acting	ditto	None
Notice of change of registered office	287	Director or secretary	Within 14 days of change	£400 + £40 daily
Notice of change in directors, secretary or in their particulars	288	ditto	ditto	£2000 + £200 daily

* The documentation listed covers the more straightforward company business. It does not include documentation which must be filed when you are involved in transactions requiring specialist legal and/or accountancy advice, for instance where application has been made to the court to vary shareholders' rights or to reduce the company's share capital.

Document	Form	Signatories	When lodged	Penalty
Contract constituting allottees' title to shares and contract of sale	—	All parties to contract	Within 14 days of change	£2000 + £200 daily
Particulars of contract 're shares allotted as fully or partly paid up otherwise than in cash	88(3)	Director or secretary	Within 1 month of allotment of shares for non-cash consideration (used when no written contract)	ditto
Return of allotments of shares	88(2)	ditto	Within 1 month of allotment	No limit on conviction on indictment. £2000 on summary conviction + £200 daily
(first) Notice of accounting reference date	224*	ditto	Within 9 months of incorporation	None but date is then 31/3
Notice of new accounting reference date	225	ditto	Before end of period	None but change ineffective
Accounts	—	Director and Director and Secretary	Within 10 months of accounting reference period	£100 to £1000 depending on delay

* This form is revoked as from 1 January 1997.

Document	Form	Signatories	When lodged	Penalty
Annual return	363a	Director or secretary	Within 28 days of the return date	£2000 + £200 daily
Special resolution	—	Director, secretary or chairman of meeting	Within 15 days of passing resolution	£1000 + £40 daily
Extraordinary resolution	—	Director, secretary or chairman of meeting	Within 15 days of passing resolution	£400 + £40 daily
Other resolution or agreement by all members or class of members not otherwise effective unless passed as special or extraordinary resolution	—	ditto	ditto	ditto
Resolution authorising increase of share capital	—	ditto	ditto	ditto
Notice of increase in nominal capital	123	Director or secretary	ditto	ditto
Notice of passing of resolution removing an auditor	386	ditto	Within 14 days of passing resolution	ditto
Notice of place where copies of directors' service contracts kept or of change in place	318	ditto	Within 14 days	ditto

Document	Form	Signatories	When lodged	Penalty
Notice of place where register of members kept or of change in place	353	ditto	ditto	ditto
Notice of place where register of holders of debentures or duplicate kept or of change in place	190	ditto	Not specified	Not specified
Notice of place where register of directors' interests in shares etc kept or of change in place	325	Director or secretary	Within 14 days	£400 + £40 daily
Particulars of mortgage or charge	395	Director, secretary, solicitor to company or mortgagee	Within 21 days of creation (instrument also to be produced)	No limit on conviction on indictment. £2000 on summary conviction + £200 daily
Particulars for registration of charge to secure series of debentures	397	Director, secretary, solicitor to company or debenture holder or their solicitor	Within 21 days of execution of trust deed or debentures (if no deed) and the deed or one debenture	ditto
Particulars of a mortgage or charge subject to which property has been acquired	400	Director or secretary	Within 21 days of acquisition	ditto

Document	Form	Signatories	When lodged	Penalty
Declaration of satisfaction in full or in part of mortgage or charge	403a	Under company seal attested as required by articles	At company's option but best lodged forthwith	ditto
Declaration that part of property or undertaking (a) has been released from charge; (b) no longer forms part of undertaking	403b	Under company seal attested as required by articles	At company's option but best lodged forthwith	No limit on conviction on indictment. £2000 on summary conviction + £200 daily.
Notice of appointment of receiver or manager	405(1)*	Person obtaining order or making appointment or their solicitor	Within 7 days of court order or appointment	£400 + £40 daily
Notice of ceasing to act as receiver or manager	405(2)*	Receiver or manager	On ceasing to act	ditto
Printed copy of memorandum as altered by special resolution	—	—	Within 15 days after period for making application to court for cancelling alteration	ditto

*Not illustrated.

Note: Documents sent to Companies House are microfilmed; forms should therefore be completed legibly and in black ink. Typed documents should be on A4 paper with a margin of not less than 10 mm (20 mm if documents are bound). Computer print is acceptable but dot matrix and carbon copy documents are not.

Accompanying cheques should be made payable to Companies House.

Fees for inspection, copies and extracts

Companies House provides public records of information filed by companies on paper, microfiche, roll film and magnetic tape and via fax (ordered by credit/debit card) and courier as well as via database direct to your PC. Credit card customers and account holders can only order by telephone, and credit card orders are subject to a minimum charge of £5.

Search-room services include standard company searches, inter-registry searches, 'history' searches (giving details of documents lodged since 1986) and premium searches. The search fee is currently £3.

Prices start from £5.50 for a microfiche copy of a company record ordered by post or telephone, £7.00 for documents ordered by post and £10.00 for copies of documents not held on microfiche. Full microfiche and roll film and magnetic tape products are also available.

Companies House also provides bulk compilations, including a list of all registered companies in Britain, a company analysis list by VAT trade classification, postcode, incorporation date or company status and a Register of Directors, Register of Disqualified Directors, Register of Registered Charges and New Incorporation Prints. More detailed analysis of the information held by Companies House is available on request.

FORMING A LIMITED COMPANY

Crown copyright. Reproduced with the permission of the Controller of Her Majesty's Stationery Office.

G

COMPANIES FORM No. 128(1)

Statement of rights attached to allotted shares

128(1)

Please do not write in this margin

Pursuant to section 128(1) of the Companies Act 1985

Please complete legibly, preferably in black type, or bold block lettering

To the Registrar of Companies
(Address overleaf)

For official use

Company number

Name of company

* insert full name of company

*

has allotted shares with rights which:

    i. are not stated in the company's memorandum or articles or in any resolution or agreement to which section 380 of the above Act applies, and

    ii. are not in all respects uniform with those attached to shares previously allotted.

† delete as appropriate

The class[es]† of such shares and the date of the first allotment of shares in each class and the rights attached to each class are:

Class of Shares	Date of first allotment
Description of Rights	

‡ Insert Director, Secretary, Administrator, Administrative Receiver or Receiver (Scotland) as appropriate

Signed   Designation‡   Date

Presentor's name address and reference (if any):

For official Use
General Section   Post room

126

G

COMPANIES FORM No. 128(3)

Statement of particulars of variation of rights attached to shares

128(3)

Pursuant to section 128(3) of the Companies Act 1985

Please do not
write in
this margin

Please complete
legibly, preferably
in black type, or
bold block lettering

To the Registrar of Companies
(Address overleaf)

For official use

Company number

* insert full name
of company

Name of company

*

§ insert date

On §_____ the rights attached to

Number of Shares	Class(es) of share

were varied as set out below (otherwise than by amendment of the company's memorandum or
articles or by any resolution or agreement to which section 380 of the above Act applies)

‡ Insert
Director,
Secretary,
Administrator,
Administrative
Receiver or
Receiver
(Scotland) as
appropriate

Signed   Designation‡   Date

Presentor's name address and
reference (if any):

For official Use	
General Section	Post room

G

COMPANIES FORM No. 128(4)

Notice of assignment of name or new name to any class of shares

128(4)

Please do not write in this margin

Pursuant to section 128(4) of the Companies Act 1985

Please complete legibly, preferably in black type, or bold block lettering

To the Registrar of Companies

For official use

Company number

Name of company

* insert full name of company

*

† delete as appropriate

gives notice of the assignment of a [new]† name or other designation to the following class[es]† of shares (otherwise than by amendment of the company's memorandum or articles or by any resolution or agreement to which section 380 of the above Act applies)

Number and class of shares	Name or other designation

‡ Insert Director, Secretary, Administrator, Administrative Receiver or Receiver (Scotland) as appropriate

Signed   Designation‡   Date

Presentor's name address and reference (if any):

For official Use

General Section   Post room

G

COMPANIES FORM No.155(6)a

Declaration in relation to assistance for the acquisition of shares.

155(6)a

Please do not write in this margin

Pursuant to section 155(6) of the Companies Act 1985

Please complete legibly, preferably in black type, or bold block lettering

To the Registrar of Companies (Address overleaf- Note 5)

For official use

Company number

Note
Please read the notes on page 3 before completing this form.

Name of company

*

* insert full name of company

I/We ø

ø insert name(s) and address(es) of all the directors

† delete as appropriate

[the sole director][all the directors]† of the above company do solemnly and sincerely declare that:

The business of the company is:

§ delete whichever is inappropriate

(a) that of a [recognised bank][licensed institution]† within the meaning of the Banking Act 1979§

(b) that of a person authorised under section 3 or 4 of the Insurance Companies Act 1982 to carry on insurance business in the United Kingdom§

(c) something other than the above§

The company is proposing to give financial assistance in connection with the acquisition of shares in the [company] [company's holding company _____ Limited]†

The assistance is for the purpose of [that acquisition][reducing or discharging a liability incurred for the purpose of that acquisition].†

The number and class of the shares acquired or to be acquired is: _____

Presentor's name address and reference (if any):

For official Use	
General Section	Post room

Page 1

155(b)a

The assistance is to be given to: (note 2) _____

The assistance will take the form of:

The person who [has acquired][will acquire]† the shares is:

† delete as appropriate

The principal terms on which the assistance will be given are:

The amount of cash to be transferred to the person assisted is £_____

The value of any asset to be transferred to the person assisted is £_____

The date on which the assistance is to be given is _____ 19 _____   Page 2

155(b)b

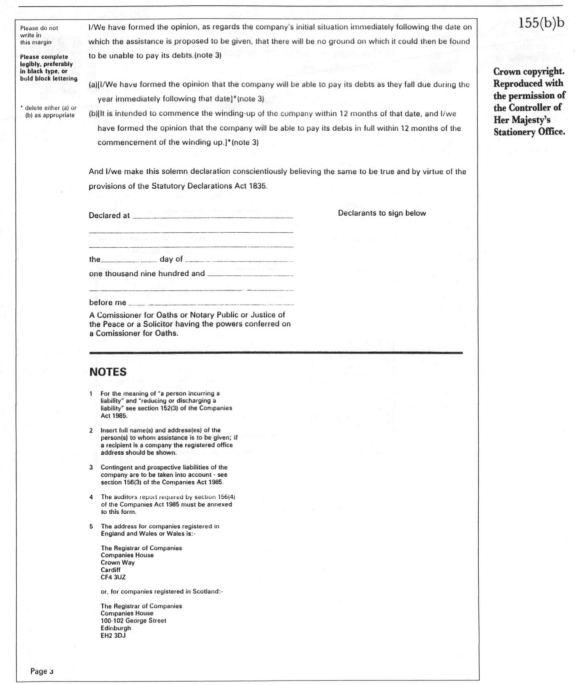

Please do not
write in
this margin

**Please complete
legibly, preferably
in black type, or
bold block lettering**

* delete either (a) or
(b) as appropriate

I/We have formed the opinion, as regards the company's initial situation immediately following the date on which the assistance is proposed to be given, that there will be no ground on which it could then be found to be unable to pay its debts.(note 3)

(a)[I/We have formed the opinion that the company will be able to pay its debts as they fall due during the year immediately following that date]*(note 3)

(b)[It is intended to commence the winding-up of the company within 12 months of that date, and I/we have formed the opinion that the company will be able to pay its debts in full within 12 months of the commencement of the winding up.]*(note 3)

And I/we make this solemn declaration conscientiously believing the same to be true and by virtue of the provisions of the Statutory Declarations Act 1835.

Declared at _____

_____

_____

the_____ day of _____

one thousand nine hundred and _____

_____

before me ____ _____

A Comissioner for Oaths or Notary Public or Justice of
the Peace or a Solicitor having the powers conferred on
a Comissioner for Oaths.

Declarants to sign below

NOTES

1 For the meaning of "a person incurring a liability" and "reducing or discharging a liability" see section 152(3) of the Companies Act 1985.

2 Insert full name(s) and address(es) of the person(s) to whom assistance is to be given; if a recipient is a company the registered office address should be shown.

3 Contingent and prospective liabilities of the company are to be taken into account - see section 156(3) of the Companies Act 1985.

4 The auditors report required by section 156(4) of the Companies Act 1985 must be annexed to this form.

5 The address for companies registered in England and Wales or Wales is:-

   The Registrar of Companies
   Companies House
   Crown Way
   Cardiff
   CF4 3UZ

   or, for companies registered in Scotland:-

   The Registrar of Companies
   Companies House
   100-102 George Street
   Edinburgh
   EH2 3DJ

Page 3

G

COMPANIES FORM No. 169

Return by a company purchasing its own shares

169

Pursuant to section 169 of the Companies Act 1985

Please do not write in this margin

Please complete legibly, preferably in black type, or bold block lettering

* insert full name of company

Note
This return must be delivered to the Registrar within a period of 28 days beginning with the first date on which shares to which it relates were delivered to the company

§ A private company is not required to give this information

‡ Insert Director, Secretary, Receiver, Administrator, Administrative Receiver or Receiver (Scotland) as appropriate

To the Registrar of Companies
(Address overleaf)

For official use

Company number

Please do not write in the space below. For Inland Revenue use only.

Name of company

*

Shares were purchased by the company under section 162 of the above Act as follows:

Class of shares			
Number of shares purchased			
Nominal value of each share			
Date(s) on which the shares were delivered to the company			
Maximum prices paid § for each share			
Minimum prices paid § for each share			

The aggregate amount paid by the company for the shares to which this return relates was: £

Stamp duty payable pursuant to section 66 of the Finance Act 1986 on the aggregate amount at 50p per £100 or part of £100   £

Signed   Designation‡   Date

Presenter's name address and reference (if any):

For official Use
General Section   Post room

132

G

COMPANIES FORM No.173

Declaration in relation to the redemption or purchase of shares out of capital

173

Please do not
write in
this margin

Pursuant to section 173 of the Companies Act 1985

Please complete
legibly, preferably
in black type,or
bold block lettering

To the Registrar of Companies
(Address overleaf - Note 4)

For official use

Company number

Name of company

* insert full name
of company

*

Note
Please read the notes
on page 2 before
completing this form.

I/We ø

ø insert name(s) and
address(es) of all
the directors

† delete as
appropriate

[the sole director][all the directors]† of the above company do solemnly and sincerely declare that:

The business of the company is:

§ delete whichever
is inappropriate

(a) that of a [recognised bank][licensed institution]† within the meaning of the Banking Act 1979§

(b) that of a person authorised under section 3 or 4 of the Insurance Companies Act 1982 to carry on
insurance business in the United Kingdom§

(c) that of something other than the above§

The company is proposing to make a payment out of capital for the redemption or purchase of its own
shares

The amount of the permissible capital payment for the shares in question is £
(note 1)

Continued overleaf

Presentor's name address and
reference (if any):

For official Use
General Section

Post room

Page 1

G

COMPANIES FORM No. 190

Notice of place where a register of holders of debentures or a duplicate is kept or of any change in that place

190

Note: This notice is not required where the register is, and has always been, kept at the Registered Office

Please do not
write in
this margin

Pursuant to section 190 of the Companies Act 1985

Please complete
legibly, preferably
in black type, or
bold block lettering

To the Registrar of Companies
(Address overleaf)

For official use

Company number

Name of company

* insert full name
of company

† delete as
appropriate

gives notice that [a register][registers]† [in duplicate form]† of holders of debentures of the company of

the classes mentioned below[is][are]† now kept at:

Postcode

Brief description of class of debentures

‡ Insert
Director,
Secretary,
Administrator,
Administrative
Receiver or
Receiver
(Scotland) as
appropriate

Signed

Designation‡

Date

Presentor's name address and
reference (if any):

For official Use

General Section

Post room

134

G

COMPANIES FORM No. 325

Notice of place where register of directors' interests in shares etc. is kept or of any change in that place

Note: This notice is not required where the register is and has always been kept at the Registered Office

325

Please do not
write in
this margin

Pursuant to section 325 of and Schedule 13 paragraph 27 to the Companies Act 1985

Please complete
legibly, preferably
in black type, or
bold block lettering

To the Registrar of Companies
(Address overleaf)

For official use

Company number

Name of company

* insert full name
of company

*

† delete as
appropriate

gives notice that the register of directors' interests in shares and/or debentures, which is kept by the company pursuant to section 325 of the above Act, is [now] † kept at:

Postcode

‡ Insert
Director,
Secretary,
Administrator,
Administrative
Receiver or
Receiver
(Scotland) as
appropriate

Signed   Designation‡   Date

Presentor's name address and
reference (if any):

For official Use
General Section

Post room

G

COMPANIES FORM No.353a

Notice of place for inspection of a register of members which is kept in a non-legible form, or of any change in that place

353a

Please do not
write in
this margin

Pursuant to the Companies (Registers and Other Records) Regulations 1985

Note: For use only when the register is kept by computer or in some other non-legible form

Please complete
legibly, preferably
in black type, or
bold block lettering

To the Registrar of Companies
(Address overleaf)

For official use

Company number

Name of company

* insert full name
of company

*

gives notice, in accordance with regulation 3(1) of the Companies (Registers and Other Records) Regulations 1985, that the place for inspection of the register of members of the company which the company keeps in a non-legible form is [now]†:

† delete as
appropriate

Postcode

Signed

[Director][Secretary]† Date

Presentor's name address and
reference (if any):

For official Use

General Section

Post room

COMPANIES FORM No. 397a

M

Particulars of an issue of
secured debentures in a series

397a

Please do not
write in
this margin

Pursuant to section 397 of the Companies Act 1985

Please complete
legibly, preferably
in black type, or
bold block lettering

To the Registrar of Companies
(Address overleaf - Note 3)

For official use

Company number

Name of company

* insert full name
of company

*

Note

Please read notes
overleaf before
completing this form

Date of present issue

Amount of present issue

Particulars as to commission, allowance or discount (note 2)

† delete as
appropriate

Signed _____ Date _____

On behalf of [company][mortgagee/chargee]†

Presentor's name address and
reference (if any):

For official Use

Mortgage Section

Post room

Time Critical Reference

M

COMPANIES FORM No. 398

Certificate of registration in Scotland or Northern Ireland of a charge comprising property situate there

398

Please do not
write in
this margin

Pursuant to section 398(4) of the Companies Act 1985

**Please complete
legibly, preferably
in black type, or
bold block lettering**

To the Registrar of Companies
(Address overleaf)

Company number

Name of company

* insert full name
of company

*

I _____

of _____

§ give date and
parties to charge

certify that the charge§ _____

of which a true copy is annexed to this form was presented for registration on _____ 19 _____

† delete as
appropriate

in [Scotland] [Northern Ireland]†

Signed

Date

Presentor's name address and
reference (if any):

For official Use
Mortgage Section

Post room

M

COMPANIES FORM No. 400

**Particulars of a charge
subject to which property
has been acquired**

400

Please do not
write in
this margin

Pursuant to section 400 of the Companies Act 1985

Please complete
legibly, preferably
in black type, or
bold block lettering

To the Registrar of Companies
(Address overleaf - Note 3)

For official use

Company number

Name of company

* insert full name
of company

*

Date and description of the instrument (if any) creating or evidencing the charge (note 1)

Amount secured by the charge _____

Names and addresses of the persons entitled to the charge

Short particulars of the property charged

Continue overleaf as necessary

Presentor's name address and
reference (if any):

For official Use
Mortgage Section

Post room

Time critical reference

Page1

139

M

COMPANIES FORM No. 403b

Declaration that part of the property or undertaking charged (a) has been released from the charge; (b) no longer forms part of the company's property or undertaking

403b

Pursuant to section 403(1)(b) of the Companies Act 1985

Please do not
write in
this margin

**Please complete
legibly, preferably
in black type or,
bold block lettering**

To the Registrar of Companies
(Address overleaf)

For official use

Company number

Name of company

* insert full name
of company

*

I, _____

of _____

† delete as
appropriate

‡ insert a description
of the instrument(s)
creating or
evidencing the
charge, eg
'Mortgage',
'Charge',
'Debenture' etc.

ø the date of
registration may be
confirmed from the
certificate

§ insert brief details
of property or
undertaking no
longer subject to
the charge

[a director][the secretary][the administrator][the administrative receiver]† of the above company, do

solemnly and sincerely declare that with respect to the charge described below the part of the property

or undertaking described [has been released from the charge][has ceased to form part of the

company's property or undertaking]†

Date and description of charge ‡ _____

Date of registration ø _____

Name and address of [chargee][trustee for the debenture holders]† _____

Short particulars of property or undertaking released or no longer part of the company's property or

undertaking § _____

_____

And I make this solemn declaration conscientiously believing the same to be true and by virtue of the

provisions of the Statutory Declarations Act 1835.

Declared at _____   Declarant to sign below

_____

_____

the _____ day of _____

one thousand nine hundred and _____

before me _____

A Commissioner for Oaths or Notary Public or Justice of
the Peace or Solicitor having the powers conferred on a
Commissioner for Oaths

Presentor's name address and
reference (if any):

For official Use	
Mortgage Section	Post room.

◀ APPENDIX 4 ▶

BOOKS, REGISTERS AND DOCUMENTS WHICH MUST BE AVAILABLE FOR INSPECTION AND OF WHICH COPIES OR EXTRACTS CAN BE REQUISITIONED

Book etc	Who can inspect	Fee	Who can requisition	Time limit for sending	Penalty
Memorandum and Articles	—	—	Any member	Not specified	£400 (company and each officer in default)
Annual Accounts, ie auditors' report, directors' report, balance sheet and profit and loss account	Copy to all members, debenture holders	None	Members and debenture holders	7 days	Unlimited fine on conviction on indictment. £2000 + £200 daily on summary conviction or £400 + £40 daily (company and each officer in default)

* To be kept at the registered office or at such other place as the directors designate.
** To be kept at the registered office.

Book etc	Who can inspect	Fee	Who can requisition	Time limit for sending	Penalty
* Accounting records	Officers at all times	None	—	—	On indictment 2 years' prison and/or fine; summary conviction 6 months' prison and/or £2000 fine + £200 daily
Book, vouchers, accounts	Auditors at all times	None	—	—	—
	Liquidator	—	—	—	On indictment 7 years' prison and/or fine; summary conviction 6 months' prison and/or £2000 fine + £200 daily
** Charge requiring registration, copy of instrument	Members and creditors	None	—	—	£400 + £40 daily
Directors' service contracts, copies, or notes of their contents	Members	None	—	—	ditto

Book etc	Who can inspect	Fee	Who can requisition	Time limit for sending	Penalty
** Minute book, general meeting	Members	None	Members	—	7 days £400; court can make order
** Register of charges	Members	None	—	—	£400 + fine
	Creditors, anyone else	Not exceeding 5p			£40 daily; court can make order
* Register of debenture holders	Members, debenture holders	None	Anyone	—	ditto
	Anyone else	Not exceeding 5p			
* Register of directors and secretaries	Members	None	—	—	£2000 fine + £200 daily
	Anyone else	Not exceeding 5p			
** Register of directors' interests	Members	None	Anyone	10 days	£400 + £40 daily
	Anyone else	Not exceeding 5p			
** Register of members and index	Members	None	Members, anyone else	Within 10 days of day after receipt of request	£400. Court can make order
	Anyone else	Not exceeding 5p			

Book etc	Who can inspect	Fee	Who can requisition	Time limit for sending	Penalty
Special resolution	—	—	Members	Not specified	£400
Extraordinary resolution	—	—	ditto	ditto	ditto
Members' resolution	—	—	ditto	ditto	ditto
Resolution for winding up	—	—	Members	ditto	ditto
Trust deed securing debenture	—	—	Debenture holders	ditto	£400 + £40 daily

Notes:
1. Penalties: Both the company and its officers can be liable for fines.
2. Memorandum: If the Memorandum is altered, the company and officers in default are liable to a fine of £200 in respect of each copy subsequently issued without the amendment.
3. Accounting Records: Officers in default have a defence if they acted honestly and the default was excusable in the circumstances, but the records must be retained for at least three years.
4. Books, vouchers and accounts: If records are inadequate or access is denied, this must be stated in the auditors' report.
5. Charges requiring registration: The instrument must be available for inspection during business hours, subject to reasonable restrictions imposed by the company in general meeting, but it must be accessible for at least two hours daily.
6. Directors' service contracts etc, the Minute book, the Register of charges, Register of debenture holders and the Register of directors and secretaries: These must be available on the same basis and the Register of directors' interests must in addition be produced at the Annual General Meeting and remain open and accessible throughout; the Register of members can, however, be closed for not more than 30 days a year, provided notice of closure is advertised in a newspaper local to the registered office.

7. Special resolution and a Resolution for winding up: If the Articles are not registered, a printed copy of the resolution must be filed. If they are registered, the resolution must be annexed to or incorporated in every copy of the Articles issued.

NOTICE OF FIRST ANNUAL GENERAL MEETING: NOTICE OF MEETING: RESOLUTIONS: MEMBERS' AGREEMENT TO SHORT NOTICE OF GENERAL MEETING AND/OR OF SPECIAL RESOLUTION: NOTES ON PRINTING OF CERTAIN DOCUMENTS: ELECTIVE RESOLUTION: FORM OF PROXY

Notice of Annual General Meeting

XYZ Limited

Notice is hereby given that the First **Annual General Meeting** of the Company will be held on _____day the ____ day of _____ 19__ at __ o'clock in the fore/after noon to transact the following business:

To receive and adopt the Accounts of the Company for the year ended ____ together with the Reports of the Directors and the Auditors.
To declare a dividend.
To re-appoint/appoint _____ as Auditors of the Company.
To fix the remuneration of the Auditors and to transact any other business which may lawfully be transacted at an Annual General Meeting.

A member entitled to attend and vote at the above meeting may appoint a proxy to attend and vote in his stead. A proxy need not be a member of the Company.

By order of the Board

Signed _____

Secretary

Notice of meeting

XYZ Limited

Notice is hereby given that an **Extraordinary General Meeting** of the above named Company will be held at _____
on _____day the _____ day of _____ 19__ at __o'clock in the fore/after noon for the purpose of considering and if thought fit passing the Resolution set out below which will be proposed as an Ordinary/Special/Extraordinary Resolution.

A member entitled to attend and vote at the above meeting may appoint a proxy to attend and on a poll* to vote in his stead. A proxy need not be a member of the Company.

By order of the Board

Signed _____

Secretary

Resolution

* If the Articles permit a proxy to vote on a show of hands, delete the words 'on a poll'.

Special resolution on change of name

Company number _____

Company name _____

At an **Extraordinary General*/Annual General*/General*** **Meeting** of the members of the above named Company duly convened and held at:

_____

_____

on the _____ day of _____ 19___
the following **Special Resolution** was duly passed:

That the name of the Company be changed to:

(new name) _____

Signature: _____ Chairman, Director, Secretary
or Officer of the Company

NB. A copy of the Resolution must be filed with the Registrar within 15 days after the passing of the Resolution.

* Delete as appropriate

Written resolution

COMPANIES ACTS

Written Resolution

Company number _____

Company name _____

We, the undersigned, being all the members of the above Company for the time being entitled to receive notice of, attend and vote at General Meetings, hereby unanimously pass the following resolution and agree that the said resolution shall for all purposes be as valid and effective as if the same had been passed at a General Meeting of the Company duly convened and held.

It is resolved that:

Dated this _____ day of _____ 19___

Signed _____

_____

_____

_____

AGREEMENT of MEMBERS to SHORT NOTICE of a GENERAL MEETING
and/or of a SPECIAL RESOLUTION

(1) 'I' or 'We'.
(2) 'Annual' or 'Extraordinary' as the case may be.

(^{1}) ———————————, the undersigned, being   member   of the above-named Company and entitled to attend and vote at the (^{2}) General Meeting of the said Company convened by a Notice of Meeting dated the   day of   19   and to be held on the   day of   19   , hereby agree that:

1.* The said meeting shall be deemed to have been duly called, notwithstanding that shorter notice than that specified in section 369 of the Companies Act 1985, or in the Company's Articles of Association, has been given therefor.

2.* The copies of the documents† referred to in sections 239 and 240 of the Companies Act 1985, which were attached to or enclosed with the said Notice of Meeting, shall be deemed to have been duly sent, notwithstanding that such copies were sent less than twenty-one days before the date of the meeting.

3.* The Special Resolution   set out in the said Notice of Meeting may be proposed and passed as   Special Resolution   , notwithstanding that less than twenty-one days' notice of such meeting has been given.

NAME (in block capitals)	ADDRESS	SIGNATURE‡

NOTES

* Delete this paragraph if not required.

† The documents referred to are the Company's profit and loss account and balance sheet, the directors' report, the auditors' report and, where the Company has subsidiaries and section 229 applies, the Company's group accounts.

‡(a) In a case where agreement is required only to the holding of an Extraordinary General Meeting, and/or to the passing of Special Resolutions at an Extraordinary General Meeting, on short notice, agreement must be given by a majority in number of the members having a right to attend and vote at the meeting, being a majority together holding not less than 95 per cent in nominal value of the shares giving a right to attend and vote at the meeting, or, in the case of a company not having a share capital, together representing not less than 95 per cent of the total voting rights at the meeting of all the members;

(b) In any other case, agreement must be given by all the members entitled to attend and vote at the meeting;

(c) One form may be signed by all the members concerned, or several similar forms may be signed by one or more of them.

Section 369 (3) and (4) of the Companies Act 1985 provide as follows:

(3) Notwithstanding that a meeting is called by shorter notice than that specified in subsection (2) or in the company's articles (as the case may be), it is deemed to have been duly called if it is so agreed:
  (a) in the case of a meeting called as the annual general meeting, by all the members entitled to attend and vote at it; and
  (b) otherwise, by the requisite majority.

(4) The requisite majority for this purpose is a majority in number of the members having a right to attend and vote at the meeting, being a majority:
  (a) together holding not less than 95 per cent in nominal value of the shares giving a right to attend and vote at the meeting; or
  (b) in the case of a company not having a share capital, together representing not less than 95 per cent of the total voting rights at that meeting of all the members.

Section 378 (2) and (3) of the Companies Act 1985 provide as follows:

(2) A resolution is a special resolution when it has been passed by such a majority as is required for the passing of an extraordinary resolution and at a general meeting of which not less than 21 days' notice, specifying the intention to propose the resolution as a special resolution, has been duly given.

(3) If it is so agreed by a majority in number of the members having the right to attend and vote at such a meeting, being a majority:
  (a) together holding not less than 95 per cent in nominal value of the shares giving that right; or
  (b) in the case of a company not having a share capital, together representing not less than 95 per cent of the total voting rights at that meeting of all the members,
  a resolution may be proposed and passed as a special resolution at a meeting of which less than 21 days' notice has been given.

Section 239 of the Companies Act 1985 provides as follows:

For the purposes of this Part, a company's accounts for a financial year are to be taken as comprising the following documents:
  (a) the company's profit and loss account and balance sheet,
  (b) the directors' report,
  (c) the auditors' report, and
  (d) where the company has subsidiaries and section 229 applies, the company's group accounts.

Section 240 of the Companies Act 1985 provides as follows:

(1) In the case of every company, a copy of the company's accounts for the financial year shall, not less than 21 days before the date of the meeting at which they are to be laid in accordance with the next section, be sent to each of the following persons:
  (a) every member of the company (whether or not entitled to receive notice of general meetings),
  (b) every holder of the company's debentures (whether or not so entitled), and
  (c) all persons other than members and debenture holders, being persons so entitled.

(2) In the case of a company not having a share capital, subsection (1) does not require a copy of the accounts to be sent to a member of the company who is not entitled to receive notices of general meetings of the company, or to a holder of the company's debentures who is not so entitled.

(3) Subsection (1) does not require copies of the accounts to be sent:
- (a) to a member of the company or a debenture holder, being in either case a person who is not entitled to receive notices of general meetings, and of whose address the company is unaware, or
- (b) to more than one of the joint holders of any shares or debentures none of whom are entitled to receive such notices, or
- (c) in the case of joint holders of shares or debentures some of whom are, and some not, entitled to receive such notices, to those who are not so entitled.

(4) If copies of the accounts are sent less than 21 days before the date of the meeting, they are, notwithstanding that fact, deemed to have been duly sent if it is so agreed by all the members entitled to attend and vote at the meeting.

Obligation to print certain documents

The Companies Act 1985

The European Communities Act 1972

1. The following documents are required to be printed:
   - (a) Articles of Association
   - (b) Altered Memorandums of Association
   - (c) Altered Articles of Association

2. The Registrar of Companies is prepared to regard the printing stipulation as satisfied by the following processes:
   Letterpress, Gravure, Lithography.
   Stencil duplicating, Offset lithography, 'Office' typeset.
   Electrostatic photocopying.
   'Photostat' or similar processes properly processed and washed.
   Stencil duplicating, using wax stencils and black ink.

3. The following documents when submitted for registration must be either printed or in a form approved by the Registrar:
   - (a) Ordinary Resolutions increasing the capital of any company.
   - (b) Special and Extraordinary Resolutions and Agreements as specified in section 380 of the Companies Act 1985.

   The Registrar is prepared to accept for registration such copy Resolutions and Agreements if produced by a process named in paragraph 2 above or by spirit duplicator, or if typed.

4. No document will be accepted if it is illegible. Where it is considered that a document, though legible, cannot be reproduced to an adequate standard for presentation to the public in microfiche or photocopy form, the Registrar's practice is to seek the co-operation of the presentor in providing a clearer copy.

5. The Registrar's present practice is to accept copies of the Memorandum and Articles amended in accordance with the following rules:

   Where the amendment is small in extent, eg a change of name or a change in the nominal capital, a copy of the original document may be amended by rubber stamp, 'top copy' typing or in some other permanent manner (but not a manuscript amendment).

   An alteration of a few lines or a complete short paragraph may be similarly dealt with if the new version is satisfactorily permanently affixed to a copy of the original in such a way as to obscure the amended words.

   Where more substantial amendments are involved, the pages amended may be removed from a copy of the original, the amended text inserted and the pages securely collated. The inserted material must be 'printed' as defined above but need not be produced by the same process as the original.

   In all cases the alterations must be validated by the seal or an official stamp of the company.

6. Where the document is produced other than by letterpress, a certificate by the printer stating the process used must be endorsed on or accompany the document.

7. It has been found by experience that documents produced by semi-dry developed dye line (diazo) copies produced by spirit duplicating or thermo-copying do not satisfy the general conditions.

Elective resolution

COMPANIES ACTS

Elective Resolution
(Pursuant to section 379A of the Companies Act 1985)

Company number _____

Company name _____

At an **Extraordinary General Meeting** of the above-named company duly convened and held at

_____

_____

on the _____ day of _____ 19___
the following Elective Resolution was duly passed:

It is resolved that:

Signed _____

NOTE: To be filed within 15 days of passing the Resolution.

Section 379A of the Companies Act 1985 provides as follows:

(1) An election by a private company for the purposes of
 (*a*) section 80A (election as to duration of authority to allot shares);
 (*b*) section 252 (election to dispense with laying of accounts and reports before general meeting);
 (*c*) section 366A (election to dispense with holding of annual general meeting;
 (*d*) section 369 (4) or 378 (3) (election as to majority required to authorise short notice of meeting); or
 (*e*) section 386 (election to dispense with appointment of auditors annually),
 shall be made by resolution of the company in general meeting in accordance with this section.
 Such a resolution is referred to in this Act as an 'elective resolution'.

(2) An elective resolution is not effective unless
 (*a*) at least 21 days' notice in writing is given of the meeting, stating that an elective resolution is to be proposed and stating the terms of the resolution; and
 (*b*) the resolution is agreed to at the meeting, in person or by proxy, by all the members entitled to attend and vote at the meeting.

(3) The company may revoke an elective resolution by passing an ordinary resolution to that effect.

(4) An elective resolution shall cease to have effect if the company is re-registered as a public company.

(5) An elective resolution may be passed or revoked in accordance with this section, and the provisions referred to in subsection (1) have effect notwithstanding any contrary provision in the company's Articles of Association.

NOTE: The Registrar of Companies is prepared to accept copy resolutions or agreements if produced to a standard which is legible and can be reproduced to an adequate standard for presentation to the public in microfiche or photocopied format. Signatures must, however, be original and *not* photocopied.

Form of proxy

Widgets Limited

I, _____ of _____

being a Member of the above named Company and entitled to vote,

hereby appoint _____ of _____

or him failing _____ of _____

as my **proxy** to attend and vote for me and on my behalf at the Annual/Extraordinary General Meeting of the Company to be held on _____day the _____ day of_____ One thousand nine hundred and _____, and at any adjournment thereof

As witness My hand this _____ day of _____ 19_____

Signed _____

in the presence of _____ *

This proxy must be deposited at the Registered Office of the Company not less than _____ hours before the time fixed for holding the above mentioned meeting.

NB. Any alterations made to the form must be initialled by the signatory and the witness.

* If the Company's Articles require the signature to be witnessed, the witness should write in his name, address and occupation.

◀ APPENDIX 6 ▶

USEFUL ADDRESSES

Association of British Chambers of Commerce
9 Tufton Street
London SW1P 3QB
0171 222 1555

Association of British Factors and Discounters
1 Northumberland Avenue
Trafalgar Square
London WC2N 5BW
0171 512 7000

Association of Company Registration Agents
20 Holywell Row
London EC2A 4JB
0171 377 0381

British Insurance & Investment Brokers Association
BIIBA House
14 Bevis Marks
London EC3A 7NT
0171 623 9043

Capital Taxes Office
England and Wales
Ferrers House
PO Box 38
Castle Meadows Road
Nottingham NG2 1BB
0115 974 2400

Northern Ireland
Law Court Building
Chichester Street
Belfast BT1 3JF
01232 235111

Scotland
16 Picardy Place
Edinburgh EH1 3NB
0131 556 8511

Central Office of Information
Hercules Road
London SE1 7DU
0171 928 2345

Chartered Association of Certified Accountants
29 Lincoln's Inn Fields
London WC2A 3EE
0171 396 5800

Chartered Institute of Arbitrators
75 Cannon Street
London EC4N 5BH
0171 236 8761

Chartered Institute of Management Accountants
63 Portland Place
London W1N 4AB
0171 637 2311

Chartered Institute of Public Finance and Accountancy
3 Robert Street
London WC2N 6BH
0171 930 3456

Confederation of British Industry (CBI)
Centre Point
New Oxford Street
London WC1A 1DU
0171 379 7400

Consumer Credit Trade Association
Tennyson House
159 Great Portland Street
London W1N 5FD
0171 636 7564

Customs and Excise
King's Beam House
39–41 Mark Lane
London EC3R 7HE
0171 626 1515

Data Protection Registration Office
Wycliffe House
Water Lane
Wilmslow
Cheshire SK9 5AF
01625 535777

Department for Education and Employment
Eighty local Training and Enterprise Councils (TECs) can offer training. Address available from your nearest Jobcentre.

Department of Trade and Industry
Financial Service and Companies' Division
Room 513
Sanctuary Buildings
16–20 Great Smith Street
London SW1P 3DB
0171 215 7877

Overseas Trade Divisions
1 Victoria Street
London SW1H 0ET
0171 215 7877

Business Links
One-stop access points for advice and support. Further information is available from your nearest TEC, Regional Government Office or Chamber of Commerce.

Designs Registry
The Patent Office
Cardiff Road
Newport
Gwent NP9 1RH
01633 814000

European Patent Office
Erhardtstrasse 27
D–8000 Munich 2
Germany

Export Credits Guarantee Department
2 Exchange Tower
PO Box 2200
Harbour Exchange Square
London E14 9GS
0171 512 7000

Finance and Leasing Association
18 Upper Grosvenor Street
London W1X 9PB
0171 491 2783

Her Majesty's Stationery Office (HMSO)
49 High Holborn
London WC1V 6HB
0171 873 0011

Hire Purchase Information Ltd
11 Grosvenor Gardens
London SW1W 0BN
0171 828 0851

Inland Revenue
Computer User Enquiries
Application Software Development
Boyd House
Lawn Central
Telford
Shropshire TF3 4HQ
01952 641146

Public Enquiry Room
West Wing
Somerset House
London WC2R 1LB
0171 438 6420/4

Superannuation Funds Office
Lynwood Road
Thames Ditton
Surrey KT7 0DP
0181 398 4242

Profit Related Pay Office
St Mungo's Road
Cumbernauld
Glasgow G67 1YZ
01236 736121

Incentive Valuation Unit
Piccadilly District
58 Conduit Street
London W1R 0DL
0171 734 7200

Institute of Chartered Accountants in England and Wales
PO Box 433
Moorgate Place
London EC2P 2BJ
0171 628 7060

Institute of Chartered Accountants in Ireland
87–89 Pembroke Road
Dublin 4
Republic of Ireland
0001 680400

11 Donegall Square South
Belfast BT1 5JE
Northern Ireland
01232 321600

Institute of Chartered Accountants of Scotland
27 Queen Street
Edinburgh EH2 1LA
Scotland
0131 225 5673

Institute of Chartered Secretaries and Administrators
16 Park Crescent
London W1N 4AH
0171 580 4741

Institute of Directors
116 Pall Mall
London SW1Y 5ED
0171 839 1233

Institute of Management
Management House
Cottingham Road
Corby
Northamptonshire
NN17 1TT
01536 204222

Insurance Ombudsman Bureau
103 New Oxford Street
London WC1A 1QH
0171 240 3838

International Chamber of Commerce
14–15 Belgrave Square
London SW1X 8PS
0171 823 2811

Land Charges Registry
The Superintendent
Land Charges Department
DX 8249, Search Section
Burrington Way
Plymouth PL5 3LP
01752 779831
(There are 13 Land Registries in England and Wales.)

Law Society, The
113 Chancery Lane
London WC2A 1PL
0171 242 1222

London Chamber of Commerce
33 Queen Street
London EC4R 1AP
(Business Registry offers advice and search facilities.)
0171 248 4444

London Enterprise Agency (LENTA)
4 Snow Hill
London EC1A 2BS
0171 236 3000

(London) Gazette
HMSO Books
PO Box 7923
London SE1 5ZH
0171 394 4580

Monopolies and Mergers Commission
New Court
48 Carey Street
London WC2A 2JT
0171 324 1467

Office of Fair Trading
Field House
Bream's Buildings
London EC4A 1PR
0171 242 2858

Licensing Branch:
Bromyard Avenue
London W3

Patent Office
Cardiff Road
Newport
Gwent NP9 1RH
01633 814000

Registrar of Companies
England and Wales
Companies House
Crown Way
Maindy
Cardiff CF4 3UZ
01222 388588

London Search Room
55–71 City Road
London EC1Y 1BB
0171 253 9393

Northern Ireland
Department of Commerce
64 Chichester Street
Belfast BT1 4JX
01232 234488

Scotland
37 Castle Terrace
Edinburgh EH1 2EB
0131 535 5800

21 Bothwell Street
Glasgow G2 6NR
0141 248 3315

Registry of County Court Judgments
171–173 Cleveland Street
London W1P 5PE
0171 380 0133

Trade Marks Registry
The Patent Office
Cardiff Road
Newport
Gwent NP9 1RH
01633 814000